CW01507500

The Devil's Coming To Get Me

The Haunting of Malvern Manor

Richard Estep

Dedicated to Mr. & Mrs. Hirzel,
James and Jennifer,
On the occasion of their wedding,

Saturday, June 16, 2018.

Wishing you a lifetime of happiness.

and

To the former residents and
caregivers of Malvern Manor

Contents

Foreword by Josh Heard

To explain how I accidentally stumbled upon Malvern Manor is quite a funny and somewhat interesting story. In the blisteringly hot days of late August 2014, I had jumped into the world of film-making; specifically, *documentary* film-making. I had written a couple of books on the subject of the paranormal, and wanted to translate one of those books into a full-length documentary. This was also proving to be quite the pain in the ass. The majority of everything that could have possibly gone wrong had done so with the grandeur of my worst nightmares. Over 75 percent of the crew had quit the project 24 hours before we were to begin filming. This was due, so they would say, to reading my book and getting spooked to the point of not wanting to continue. A few other set-backs were looming around and presenting their ugly faces on occasion as well. Set-backs such as funding and my father being hospitalized during the first day of filming. These all took their own toll on me throughout the first few days of filming *A Brush With Evil.*

I wanted to begin *A Brush With Evil* with a ghost hunt. A broad-stroke view of who we were as a team and how we conducted investigations of paranormal activity. The opening scene of the film was to take place at a small diner in Malvern, Iowa called The Classic Café. "The Classic," as I call it, serves the small town of Malvern well, offering a big-city feel with hospitality generously sprinkled on top. It also has a slew of paranormal happenings. Not that anyone in town really knows much about that. The Classic was also generous enough to allow us to film our opening scene and investigation there. But I had forgotten one small detail; a detail that is crucial to any investigation: noise contamination. There is a bar that is attached to The Classic and somehow I spaced this small detail off at some point. Maybe it was the funding crap, my father, or the crew jumping ship on the rest of us, but there it was staring me directly in the face. Patrons and locals laughing and having a great time with a lexicon of libations flowing like a summer stream. We were hosed.

I walked outside calmly, but inside I was fuming. I sparked the first of what would become 4 cigarettes over the course of only 15 minutes or so. While extinguishing the first cigarette, I heard a voice from beside me ask, "What's with all the cameras?" I politely replied that we were filming a documentary. The gentleman, who was dressed nicely and was wearing a smile asked, "About what?" I explained that,

"This is where I typically lose people, but it's a documentary on the paranormal." At this point, you either spark up a conversation or the person may look at you like your own mother doesn't love you. I was happy to see his general interest in the subject.

Quincy was the name of the new face I had just met. Quincy also had quite a story to tell. He explained to me that he owned a creepy building where some fairly odd things occur from time to time. "Sure they do" was the only thing that came to my mind. I've only heard this one roughly 10,000 times in the past few years. But what he had to say was incredible!

Quincy quickly launched into a narrative that I had no idea I would soon be regurgitating to others on a daily basis. He told me that the structure itself was originally a hotel. Built in the late 1800's and widely popular with traveling businessmen on the railroad, the Cottage Hotel was the place to be in the sleepy town of Malvern. In the 1950's the building began serving the community as more of what we would consider to be a nursing home. Primarily it serviced the elderly who could no longer take care of themselves. This however was fairly short-lived because when the 1970's rolled around the state of Iowa came in and stated that the hallways weren't wide enough to properly transport patients throughout the facility.

This is where history becomes the most fascinating for geeks and nerds such as myself. This point in history is when the nursing home becomes a care facility that would service any type of mental disability that one could fathom. Everyone from addicts, alcoholics, and people with Down's Syndrome to some very exotic cases of multiple personalities (now known as Dissociative Identity Disorder), schizophrenics, and even murders were calling this place home. This was a very odd population of people co-existing under the same roof. Especially by today's standards. What fascinates me the most about the clientele is that the population remained the same up until closing in the early months of 2005.

Quincy was kind enough to let us in the building that night for the purposes of filming. He really saved our rumps. But I didn't realize the amount of activity that was waiting for us inside this 10,000 square foot structure. It was almost as if we couldn't point the cameras in the correct direction fast enough. There were disembodied voices, knocks and bangs that would confuse and send us all running in different directions, and roughly a dozen personal experiences that cannot be explained to this day. I was absolutely hooked to say the very least.

My first experience at the manor was fortunately captured on video as well. We were upstairs in what we call the "short hallway." This hallway has a lot going on to say the very least. Obviously, during filming we didn't know specific history. That would take months to gather and correlate. A member of the film crew, my brother James and I were all hearing a noise coming from room 17. Upon further investigation, we began to hear footsteps in the hallway and a strange moaning noise coming from inside of room 17. We heard these phenomenon a few times, almost as if it was warning us to leave. Just as we were about to leave the room, I started to experience something very odd. I was getting a very sharp pain in my back. Not like a muscle pull or anything like that. This was new and something that I have never felt before; more like a burning sensation. All I know for sure is that it hurt like hell. My brother was yelling at me to get out of the room but I honestly couldn't focus on anything other than the pain in my back. It was sharp and very painful. This was the very moment I realized that this house wasn't screwing around and was most certainly not for the faint of heart.

After concluding the film project, I kept in contact with Quincy and talked to him about the building itself. I explained to him that a place of that caliber is something that is hard to find within the paranormal community and he should consider opening the doors to the public. Quincy considered it briefly and agreed with me. Within a couple of months, the doors would be officially open to paranormal investigators, researchers, and thrill-seekers alike. We ended up calling it Malvern Manor so it could stand on its own and not be associated with any other business or former owner from its long and history-packed past.

The guests would come and pay the money for their time. I would collect, give the tours, and run the money over to Quincy at the day's end. And then one day, it quickly became apparent that the Manor's days could be numbered. I received a phone call from Quincy. He explained to me that he was offered a new job and was going to accept the position. This coincidentally would mean that he needed to move to another town and ultimately put the Manor up for sale. I could literally feel my stomach in my throat during this conversation. Roughly five hundred scenarios raced through my brain as Quincy was still talking to me. The most predominate of these thoughts was the doors ultimately closing and the Manor and land it sat on being converted into a parking lot. Luckily that never happened and I was fortunate enough to find some like-minded people who were willing to go into this venture with me and try to make a run of it. This has been one of my biggest blessings.

To this day we still give daily tours and overnight investigations. The rooms and furnishings are precisely as we found them on the first night that we accidentally stumbled upon what we now call Malvern Manor. I feel that it adds a little more to the integrity of the place from an investigative standpoint.

Looking back at everything that has happened since that first night of finding the manor, it puts an odd, boyish grin on my face. Was this something that was meant to be? Did this building, this location choose this path? Was this something that was meant for me personally? I honestly wish I had the answer to any one of these questions. But I will say this, I no longer believe in simple coincidences.

Josh Heard
Malvern, Iowa
March 2018

Introduction

It was dark and silent in the nursing home hallway. The last residents had departed years ago, their empty rooms long since abandoned. In the middle of the long corridor could be found the remnants of the nurses' station. Most of the structure had been ripped out, but a series of wooden pigeon-holes still remained, each with the name of the last owner still inscribed on the front. They had once been used to store medications and paperwork, but now contained nothing but dust.

Standing close to the nurses' station was a man. Johnny Houser was acutely aware that he was currently the only flesh-and-blood occupant of Malvern Manor. A seasoned paranormal investigator of many years' experience, Houser was not a man who was easily frightened or intimidated. He had a unique day job: Living next door to the infamous Villisca Ax Murder House, roughly an hour's drive away from Malvern, he was both caretaker and subject matter expert on what was widely regarded as one of the country's most haunted houses.

Although a team player, Houser adopted a lone wolf

approach for the TV show he was working on. *Johnny Houser Vs.* saw him visiting a different haunted location each episode and spending time investigating it completely on his own, without a crew or fellow investigators to back him up. It was a ballsy thing to do, but spending countless hours all by himself inside the Ax Murder House was undoubtedly good training to prepare him for it.

He had no idea that Malvern Manor was about to give him a little more than he had bargained for.

Johnny was a pretty low-key sort of guy. Before conducting anything like a formal paranormal investigation, he liked to take a wander through the corridors and rooms of the location he was investigating, just soaking up the atmosphere and getting a general feel for the place. He had already explored the main part of the building, and had then moseyed on over to the old nursing home wing.

Stories abounded of a Shadow Man who was said to haunt one end of the long hallway. Visitors had found themselves getting rushed by a tall, dark figure, always in the same location – the exact same spot in which Johnny was now standing.

Although there were a few lights still working in the nursing home wing, Johnny had deliberately left them switched off. It took a while for his eyes to adjust to the dark, but when they did, he was easily able to make out the rectangular shapes of doorways on either side of the corridor, spaced at regular intervals. His attention was focused on Room 2, at the far end of the corridor on the right. This was said to be the domain of what people were now starting to refer to as the Shadow Man.

Johnny stood there long enough for him to lose track of the time. All about him was quiet and peaceful. His eyes roamed all around, looking for signs that he might not really be alone in there. Still nothing stirred.

He was about to give up and relocate. Then it happened. The Shadow Man seemed to come out of nowhere. One minute, the end of the hallway was nothing more than an empty pool of shadow; the next, a tall, blacker-than-black figure was standing there. Johnny stared at the Shadow Man, hardly able to believe what his eyes were seeing. The figure stared right back at him, seeming to size him up somehow.

Then it charged.

Even though he'd been halfway expecting something like this to happen, Johnny still somehow found himself caught off guard. The idea of going for his phone to take a photograph never even crossed his mind. He was rooted to the spot, unable to move a muscle as the Shadow Man bore down on him. The figure moved much too quickly for a human being, covering the entire distance between them in the space of just two heartbeats. All that Johnny could manage to do was brace himself for impact.

It was an impact that never came. When the dark figure reached a point just a few short inches in front of his face, it disappeared into thin air, melting away just as quickly as it had appeared. For just a second, Johnny simply stood there, his heart pounding away in his chest like a jackhammer.

Then he did what almost anybody else would have done under the same circumstances. He turned and ran out of there as fast as his legs would carry him.

My name is Richard Estep. I've been a paranormal investigator since 1995, researching cases of purported hauntings on both sides of the Atlantic. Many of those cases turned out to have an entirely mundane and everyday explanation, but some did not, and it's that relatively small percentage of seemingly inexplicable occurrences that keep me coming back for more.

Malvern Manor first popped up on my radar when I saw it on TV. The episode of *Paranormal Lockdown* in which Nick Groff, Katrina Weidman, and camera operator Rob Safi spent 72 hours shut inside the now-abandoned former care facility was intriguing, and I remember thinking at the time that it should go on my paranormal investigator's bucket list. (That's a long list, by the way, and it seems to grow longer with every passing year...)

On Halloween night of 2017, I was spending the week investigating one of my favorite haunted locations in the world, the old Tooele Valley Hospital just outside Salt Lake City in Utah. Now a full contact haunted house attraction named Asylum 49, the former hospital kindly allows me to move in each year with a team of fellow paranormal investigators in an attempt to unlock some of its many secrets.

A sister team had joined us. Named AAPI (short for the American Association of Paranormal Investigators) this was a small group who generally punched well above their weight when they were working a case. One of their investigators was a good personal friend of mine. In addition to being a world-class cellist and Catholic priest, Stephen also happened to be a highly-skilled paranormal investigator. He and I had worked together for over a decade, spending nights in haunted jails, fire houses, hospitals, and during one particularly memorable week, a prison for those who were once accused of witchcraft. I trusted and respected both Stephen and his team-mates implicitly, and would soon come to consider all of them friends.

Contrary to what you may have seen on television, there is a lot of downtime during an investigation. We were all sitting around enjoying a break from our experiments and getting our obligatory caffeine fix. Conversation soon turned to the subject of what cases we all had on the horizon.

"Don't forget," said Erik, "we have Malvern Manor coming up next spring. Last time we went, the activity there was insane."

My ears instantly perked up. "Malvern Manor – that's the place from *Paranormal Lockdown*, right?"

"Right," Stephen nodded. It was so active last time, we got some great evidence."

They started to tell me about their past experiences at Malvern Manor, including what they considered to be their crowning achievement – capturing video footage on an SLS camera of what appeared to be a small stick figure hanging in one of the upstairs closets. I was practically salivating by the time they were done. Stephen must have noticed and taken pity on me, because he asked me whether I'd like to accompany them on their return visit.

Oh, *hell* yes.

Fast-forward approximately five months, and I'm in a rented SUV with Stephen, Erik, and Jill, making the eight hour drive from my adopted state of Colorado to Iowa. Along with two fellow investigators, we were going to take over Malvern Manor for ninety-six hours. Over that four-day period we would leave no stone unturned in our attempt to gather and document evidence of the haunting, and it is very safe to say that Malvern Manor did not disappoint.

The book you are now reading chronicles not only our investigation, but also the experiences of many others who have braved those haunted hallways. The sources of these accounts range from personal interviews to the contents of the Malvern Manor guest book, a plain-looking notebook in which visitors are invited to write down in their own words the events which befell them during the course of their visit. Some of the stories are frankly incredible, and a number of them are downright terrifying. It should go without saying that I can only vouch for those events that I personally witnessed during the course of my own stay at Malvern Manor. With that being said, it is fascinating to note just how often and consistently people who have never met one another claim to experience phenomena that is either identical or at the very least, remarkably similar.

On that note, I recommend that you sit back and relax. It is time for us to go and meet the spirits of Malvern Manor.

Richard Estep   Longmont, Colorado   May 2018

Chapter One
Locked Down

The episode of *Paranormal Lockdown* set at Malvern Manor opens with a brief overview of the building's colorful history. Hosts Nick Groff and Katrina Weidman were advised to visit Malvern Manor by fellow paranormal investigator Johnny Houser, who would come to play a pivotal role in their investigation...and, although I had no way of knowing when I sat down to watch it on TV, my own investigation as well.

They are met by Josh Heard, who tells them about the role of one Captain Cullers being instrumental in the upkeep of the Manor, and the fact that he is often heard to this day, a gruff, deep male voice distinctly referring to himself as "the Captain."

Next up is Gracie's room, where Josh advises them that Gracie prefers to interact with male investigators, tugging on their clothing and striking the walls when they attempt to leave. Nick claims that he can sense a great deal of energy and confusion in the room.

Heading upstairs, their first stop is Inez's room. Not

knowing any better at the time, Josh lays out the story of Inez's death, mistakenly claiming that it took place in that very room. Only later would he learn that Inez had in fact died elsewhere in town.

Making their way up to the attic, Nick Groff claims that there is evidence of a fire which "killed at least one resident of the Manor." Distinct charring is still visible around the eaves, rafters, and the apex of the roof. They are interrupted by an odd sound in one of the enclosed spaces, which they are unable to debunk. Without seeing more footage, it's difficult to say whether the sound was caused by the tree branches outside scraping against the roof, which I learned first-hand creates some pretty eerie noises in the attic, or whether it had some other explanation.

No sooner has Josh locked them in the building for 72 hours than Katrina begins to feel sick in the parlor. Johnny Houser arrives and takes them over to the nursing home wing, relating his experience with the Shadow Man. They are interrupted by what sounds like a knock or a footstep from the far end of the nursing home wing hallway, from the direction of Room 2. Now Johnny begins to feel dizzy and light-headed too, for no apparent reason.

Nick knocks on the door of Room 2 while Johnny

challenges the Shadow Man to come on out, sadly to no avail. Johnny heads home, leaving Nick, Katrina, and Rob all alone inside the building.

As their first night begins, Nick and Katrina elect to begin with the Shadow Man's hallway, setting up a grid of red lasers to help detect its presence. They leave cameras running and then relocate to Inez's room, attempting to interact with the little girl's spirit. They begin an ITC (Instrumental Trans-Communication) session in the hallway, getting responses that sound somewhat like *Hello, Hi,* and *Let me help you.* It's always important to bear in mind that audio pareidolia is rife when it comes to such devices; the human brain wants to make sense of random, chaotic sounds, and is very adept at deluding itself into thinking that garbled noise is really a form of language. With that being said, I have seen such devices deliver spectacular results on occasion, and I am still an advocate of using them...with a certain degree of healthy skepticism, that is.

Nick and Katrina choose their sleeping spots for the night. Katrina very bravely opts for the Shadow Man's hallway, reasoning that by making herself vulnerable (being sick, tired, and sleepy) may draw him out; Nick goes for Gracie's room, where he felt some kind of energy during their initial walk-through. After spending four days at the Manor, I would have been willing to sleep in Gracie's room, but would have felt distinctly uncomfortable bedding down in the nursing home wing. My hat goes off to Katrina for doing so.

Nick had left a voice recorder running overnight. The phrase, *Nick, get up,* was recorded, followed by, *Hello Nick*! being screamed loudly into the mic.

Using the SLS camera in the hallway outside Inez's room, Nick tries to make contact with her while Katrina monitors the screen. A transient cold draft drifts between two of the rooms, then a loud thump is heard elsewhere in the building. Then they hear what sounds like something being dragged in one of the second-floor rooms. They localize the noise to a closet, and replicate it by running a fingernail along the wall.

Another loud thud. Katrina feels as if she is being watched. Nick thinks that he hears a man speaking, and Katrina posits that this could possibly be the Captain.

"Captain Cullers, can you give us a sign that you're here with us?" Nick asks. Yet another bang, this one seeming to emanate from downstairs, and Nick says that his arms feel "all staticky."

Katrina suspects that the Captain is behind all this, and begins calling out to him, but he doesn't seem to want to interact any longer. The standard Malvern Manor 'cat and mouse' game – a phrase that you will see repeated in this book again and again – is now in full swing.

With night two upon them, Nick and Katrina set up an EVP experiment in the attic. Katrina sleeps in the parlor this time, choosing an old leather chair in lieu of a bed. Nick goes for the hallway upstairs.

The voice recorder that was left running overnight in the attic has captured some fascinating EVP results, including a voice that appears to say, *Johnny Houser... He will come back.* Again, assuming that this is not audio pareidolia, this makes for an impressive result indeed. Our own investigation would also yield similar results, with Johnny's name coming across through the speakers in Hank's room.

In addition to Johnny Houser's name being spoken, the name *Inez* also emerges. Somewhat more disturbing is that the name seems to be said by the voice of a man, not that of a little girl.

Operating the SLS camera in the hallway outside the Shadow Man's room, Katrina is surprised to see an adult-sized stick figure flash into existence next to Nick, only to disappear almost instantly.

Johnny Houser returns to lend them a little energy. Standing outside Room 2, Johnny is startled when his wireless microphone, which was clipped to his belt line, is pulled to the floor. Johnny is left all alone at the end of the Shadow Man's hallway, and tries to entice the entity to come out. He hears a whisper of some kind, then footsteps at the opposite end of the hallway. Right on the heels of that, something touches him on the shoulder, startling him.

The ITC device says that *Johnny is here.*

Trying to locate the source of the footsteps, Johnny heads down to Room 7, where is he overcome with intense sadness. This room is well-known to be haunted by the spirit of a lady who dislikes the company of males but seems drawn to other women.

Having gone upstairs in order to prevent the noise from contaminating Johnny's efforts, Nick and Katrina once again attempt to contact Captain Cullers. "Do you know where Inez is, the little girl?" Nick wants to know. The answer comes in the form of a single, chilling word: *Here.*

You're talking to me, the box says, before adding, *Second floor.* A number of other possibly intelligent responses also come through before the three investigators reunite in the Shadow Man's hallway.

It had been an eventful and tiring 72 hours for Nick, Katrina, and Johnny. Intrigued by what I had seen, I could only hope that our own experience would be every bit as fruitful.

We had no idea.

Chapter Two
First Impressions

It was roughly a nine hour drive from eastern Colorado to the western border of Iowa, with a couple of rest stops factored in. Stephen, Erik, Jill and I all traveled down together. The rest of our team, Susan and Connie, would be coming in from different states, and making their own way to Malvern.

I have already mentioned my friendship with Stephen, our resident paranormal investigator slash priest slash cellist. I always like to think of him as the equivalent of spiritual heavy artillery – in fact, he was the first and only person I called when it appeared that I had brought some kind of attachment back to my own home. When my wife and I heard disembodied voices, saw a shadow figure in broad daylight, and (the final straw) watched in horror as a number of glass picture frames decided to jump off the fireplace, almost landing on our cat, I finally decided that enough was enough. Stephen came on over and conducted some kind of blessing/banishment combination that was intended to get rid of our uninvited guest for good. It worked like a charm, and he didn't even give me a hard time for being agnostic. Talk about great customer service! If you picture a thinner version of Benjamin Franklin in your mind – albeit a version of him that happens to be wearing luminous neon green running shoes – then you have a pretty good mental picture of Stephen.

I hadn't done many investigations with Jill, but from what little work we had done together, I really liked her approach to the field. Although more than adept at using the vast array of tools and gadgets that most teams like to deploy these days, much like Stephen, she combined the technical aspect with a strong sensitivity to the spiritual side of things. As the investigation went on, I would learn that Jill made a great barometer for just how active or inactive a particular part of the Manor would be at any given moment.

Last, but by no means least, was Erik. He bore a striking resemblance to the bearded Luke Skywalker from *Star Wars Episode VIII: The Last Jedi,* and spoke in a voice that was uncannily like that of Brian, the talking dog from the TV show *Family Guy.* With an extensive background in the field of information technology, Erik knew his tech cold. In addition to being a skilled and experienced investigator, Erik was also an accomplished author and narrator of several audio books. He was a real trooper, having driven the four of us all the way from Colorado to Iowa without giving anybody else a shot at the wheel.

We'd started out at ten o'clock in the morning. The sun was just going down when we arrived in Malvern.

As a kid growing up in England during the 1970s and 1980s, I had seen a lot of movies that took place in towns like Malvern; to me, it looked like the quintessential American small town, centered around a main street that housed various shops and small businesses.

"We're nearly there," Erik said, mostly for my benefit. My three companions had been here before, but this was to be my first time investigating Malvern Manor, and I was equally thrilled and nervous about doing so; thrilled because of the place's fearsome reputation, and nervous because of...well, the place's fearsome reputation. I had read and heard so many accounts of the paranormal activity that people had claimed to experience at the Manor, and while all of them were fascinating, some were a definite cause for concern.

For example, when she heard that I would be spending a few days at the Manor, a friend wrote to me and told me to be careful because when she visited for a brief tour, she took home some kind of spirit attachment, which turned out to be very difficult for her to get rid of.

"Something like that happened to me the last time I was here," Erik said when he told him the news. "It was more than a little disturbing."

He had been driving away from Malvern Manor and heading back to his hotel at the end of a long night spent investigating the place, when suddenly he sensed that he was not alone in the car. While there were no other flesh and blood passengers in the vehicle, he was overcome with the sudden conviction that there was a definite presence sitting directly behind him. Glancing up to check the rear-view mirror, all had appeared quiet and empty back there.

Without warning, he felt an ice-cold sensation wash over him.

"Oh, hell no," Erik insisted vehemently, talking out loud to an apparently empty car. "You are not going anywhere with me. You are going back to Malvern Manor, right now!"

Whoever this 'phantom hitch-hiker' was, they seemed willing to obey Erik's command. The feeling dissipated as quickly as it had arrived, and Erik was only too happy to be left all on his lonesome again.

Erik is an experienced paranormal investigator and a

very down-to-Earth kind of guy, not prone to making up stories or indulging in fantasies about the locations he investigates. The fact that his experience dovetailed so neatly with that of my other friend was extremely interesting. It made me wonder just how many other visitors to Malvern Manor ended up inadvertently taking an unwanted spirit attachment away with them when they left the place. I immediately resolved to have Stephen, our resident Catholic priest, take whatever protective measures he could during our time there. The last thing I wanted was to let an unwanted entity into my home.

And speaking of Malvern Manor, there it was, off to our left. A burger joint screened some of it from the main street, but I could still make out most of the upper floor and the roof. Erik turned left, pulling the car over to the side of the road directly in front of the building. We all got out of the car and stood in the street, just taking in the sight of the haunted old building we had come so far to visit. The Manor appeared to be a dark and foreboding place, but how much of that was genuine and how much was entirely psychological, the sort of thing that was easily attributable to the many ghost stories and legends that surrounded the place?

Only an in-depth investigation would tell for sure.

Making full use of what little daylight remained, the four of us took it in turns to snap pictures of the building. I half-expected to look up and see a face or a figure looking back at us from somewhere inside the Manor, but the windows were all dark and devoid of any signs of life.

"Let's go and have a look around," Stephen suggested. We weren't going to get the keys until the following morning, but there was no harm in walking around the outside of the building and taking a few photos of the exterior, especially after coming all this way. Looking left and right for oncoming traffic, the priest crossed the street and led us toward the front of the Manor.

It was immediately apparent that Malvern Manor had seen better days. The paint was chipped and peeling in places, and there was a general sense of age and decay to the building. Lest that be interpreted as criticism by the reader, I should make clear that in my view, the fact that Josh and his colleagues are able to keep the place open at all is nothing short of a miracle; if they had not stepped in and bought the place, making it a going concern once more, the place would have been long since abandoned and left derelict – or worse still, demolished.

We soon came to the porch on which residents often used to sit and enjoy the sun. A number of old chairs had been left out there for modern day visitors to sit on. Heading around the side of the building and circling round to the back, we passed a couple of exterior wooden staircases that had been blocked off and covered up with crime scene tape – not because a crime had taken place there, I hasten to add, but because the wood had rotted to such an extent that the staircases were structurally unsafe and therefore too dangerous to use.

The four of us were standing on the rear side of the Manor, taking photographs of the back aspect, when a car pulled onto the lot and stopped right in front of us. The man who got out bore a striking resemblance to the actor Kiefer Sutherland.

"Hi Josh," Erik said, shaking hands with what turned out to be one of Malvern Manor's owners. I'd seen Josh on *Paranormal Lockdown,* and was happy to find that he was every bit as friendly and affable in real life as he appeared on TV.

"I'm just here to check the water meter," Josh

explained, fishing around in his pocket and finally producing a set of keys. "We got a massive water bill this month, but there's no sign of a leak. I think it may be a faulty meter. Would you guys like to have a look around while you're here?"

Would we ever! Josh unlocked the back door and led us inside. The door opened into a surprisingly spacious kitchen. This was by no means a comprehensive tour – that would come the following afternoon – but just a taster for now. He wandered from room to room, flipping on lights as he went. I noticed that most of the windows were covered with sheets of black plastic, which seemed to be doing a pretty good job of keeping out most of the ambient light from the street outside.

I walked into a wood-paneled room at the front of the building and found a pair of wheelchairs sitting side by side. I wasn't sure whether they had originally belonged to the Manor or not, and made a mental note to ask Josh about them later – and perhaps spend some time sitting in one while conducting an EVP session.

If this had been a horror movie, I would be telling you about the deep sense of foreboding and dread that suddenly came over me during those first few minutes inside

Malvern Manor. The truth was that yes, the place was a little creepy, but how much of that was simply my own active imagination working against me? I'd heard plenty of stories about the place, and there was also the fact that it looked old and abandoned inside – it would have been remarkable if the place wasn't haunted. But I certainly wasn't feeling any negative or ominous overtones on that first, brief flying visit.

I stood for a moment at the foot of the staircase, gazing up into the darkness of the second floor. Again, I didn't feel anything unusual while I was standing there – it would only be later that I would get some disturbing warnings about that particular part of the Manor, and my fellow investigators would experience something they would really rather forget.

Josh told us that he had to go on down to the basement to make doubly sure that there were no leaks. As the basement/cellar was separate from the rest of the Manor and not somewhere that visitors usually got to go, I seized on the opportunity to ask him if he'd like some company.

"Sure," he agreed, and five minutes later we were back outside watching him unlock the big double doors that led to the cellar steps. The staircase was steep and fairly narrow, but thankfully there was a handrail for safety's sake.

Just as one would expect, the basement was dank and claustrophobic, smelling of soil and wood. It was criss-crossed with pipes and conduits that forced us to duck in order to avoid hitting our heads. Josh took the lead and went straight to the back of the basement, checking for water leaks along each stretch of pipe. There were none to be found, and certainly nothing to explain the massive amounts of water that the utility bill claimed the Manor was getting through each month. None the wiser, we made our way carefully back up into the fresh air again.

"We have a private tour tomorrow morning, but then the place is yours until Sunday," Josh said, locking the building up again. "Come on by any time."

Thanking him, we went back to our rental car and headed for our accommodation for the night. Stephen and Jill were staying in a bed and breakfast two blocks away, a beautiful old church that dated back to the 1800s. Erik and I had gone the more conventional route of getting hotel rooms a little further out.

Before turning in for the night, the four of us talked about the Manor in general. Jill and Stephen had both felt a little wary in some parts of the building, but the conversation soon turned to the staircase that led up to the second floor.

Jill told me about a fellow member of their team, a psychic medium named Colton. Although I am generally wary of those who purport to have psychic capabilities (until they have proven their abilities to some degree, at least) Stephen, Jill, and Erik all insist that Colton has been almost scarily accurate with a number of his findings.

After their last visit to Malvern Manor, the AAPI team members had shown him some of the photographs they had taken over the course of their investigation. Almost immediately, he insisted that someone – or some*thing* – had been standing at the bottom of the staircase, silently watching them leave. It was "just checking them out," Colton had said, and finished with a rather chilling warning: when (not if, but when) they returned to Malvern Manor in the future, it would still be there, waiting for them.

What was this entity's nature and intent? "It is something very large," he had expanded, "very negative, and it definitely doesn't have anyone's best interests at heart but its own. And it feeds off the fear of those who visit."

To be one hundred percent honest, while I was very receptive to what my colleagues were telling me, I was also going to take it with a healthy grain of salt, considering the source. Without some more tangible form of proof, I would never be able to tell if there was a legitimate concern here or just the impressions of a single individual, and one who had never visited Malvern Manor in person at that.

Erik and I dropped Stephen and Jill off at their AirBnB and drove back to our hotel. It was getting on for midnight, and we all wanted to get a good night's sleep in so that we could start out our first proper day of investigation feeling fresh and well-rested. I had posted a few of my photographs of the Manor exterior on social media. Before turning in for the night, I scrolled through the comments and found something interesting that had been posted by a friend from back in Colorado.

> *Oh my. I didn't see who posted these photos at first, but at first glance I felt a really sick sensation in the pit of my stomach. I got the feeling as if something really bad went down there. I couldn't even keep looking at the photos.*

The poster went on to say that she was convinced that there was something extremely dark and negative haunting that location, that it had fed upon those residents of the Manor that had been mentally ill, treated them as if they were puppets, and had perhaps even emotionally tortured them. She had no hesitation in calling out this entity as being downright evil, and concluded by saying that I had best be very careful.

Her comments bore striking similarities to those made by Colton, and it struck me as being rather odd to say the least that two individuals, neither of whom knew the other, had told such a similar story based purely upon photographs of Malvern Manor.

A dark, malicious spirit entity of some description. Surely they both had to be exaggerating...didn't they?

Chapter Three

Inez

Everybody slept late the following morning. The day was gray and overcast when Stephen, Erik, Jill, and I drove into Malvern.

After a hearty brunch at a lovely little cafe across the street from Malvern Manor, we walked up to the building a little before two o'clock in the afternoon. Josh Heard was there to meet us. A private tour was just finishing up, warning us that they had "been a little provocative" upstairs and might have stirred things up a little for us. Generally speaking, my philosophy is not to provoke during a paranormal investigation if possible – I think that it shows a lack of respect for the spirits of the decent people that once lived and worked there – but there have been exceptions; for example, at Fox Hollow Farm in Carmel, Indiana, I made a point of very aggressively calling out the spirit of serial killer Herbert Baumeister, otherwise known as the I-70 Strangler. I really didn't feel the need to show any respect to a man who had murdered at least eleven young men in the basement of that location. I wasn't going to provoke at Malvern, but it looked as though the decision had been made already by the visiting group of tourists.

As one might expect, Josh possesses a wealth of knowledge concerning both the paranormal field in general (he's a seasoned and accomplished investigator) and Malvern Manor in particular, including its history and haunting.

Before we could get to that, however, came the necessary business of each investigator signing individual waivers in order to be allowed to spend time at the Manor.

"I think our lawyer had some fun with this," Josh laughed, passing over the single-sheet waivers to us to sign. It was quite unlike any legal document that I have ever been asked to sign before. It is reproduced here in full:

> *I understand that I am in a place with significant reported paranormal activity, and while such has not been scientifically proven, I will NOT hold the ownership or management liable or responsible in any way for psychological experiences or effects, whether long term or short term. I acknowledge that I have not disclosed my psychological condition, state of mind, or physical condition with any degree of certainty, and I take full responsibility and assume all risks for any effect that this may have on*

my state of mind, mental health, and physical effects. If I am a minor, parental consent is **REQUIRED.**

I understand that I am possibly going to be in dimly lit areas, without total control of my whereabouts, and that I will take **FULL** *responsibility and assume* **ALL** *risks of personal injury from where I go, how I walk, and how I conduct myself during the event. I know I am free to leave and I understand that I will not be held against my will by management and will report such if any other guest does so or attempts to do so. I will not hide in the bathrooms or use them for anything other than using the toilet for its intended purpose. I understand that management retains the responsibility to provide a safe structure for all the guests, but has no control or responsibility if events occur or reactions ensue caused by the paranormal. I will not lean over railings or put my body weight anywhere where a stair or railing could break. I will be held liable if I break anything or cause damage in a panic. I understand that if I act unruly or do not respect the rights and experiences of others, I may be warned to*

leave, or asked to immediately leave, without
admission cost refunds, if harm is caused.

It was definitely one of the more eclectic legal documents that I'd ever been asked to affix my signature to. The only one that came anywhere close was the waiver for Asylum 49, a full-contact haunted house attraction in Tooele, Utah...which also happens to be extremely haunted. That particular waiver requires a fingerprint in addition to a signature.

I duly signed it with a flourish.

While each of us was scanning through the legalese on the waiver forms, Erik asked Josh about the dire predictions made by Colton and my Facebook friend – in his opinion, Erik wanted to know, was there really a dark entity haunting Malvern Manor, and if so, was it something that we should be afraid of?

Josh thought about it for a moment and framed his response carefully. "There's one thing about this place that fascinates me above everything else, and it's to do with the whole story of Inez." Inez was, of course, the 12 year-old girl who was said to have hanged herself in a room at the end of the hallway up on the second floor, and now supposedly haunts Malvern Manor in general and that room in particular. Yet it appears that there is more to the story of Inez than first meets the eye.

Inez May Gibson was born on August 6th, 1888. Her adoptive father (who was also her uncle) worked as a grocer in Malvern, and had taken Inez in when her parents had gotten a divorce without either one of them being willing to accept responsibility for their own children.

While hardly the recipe for a happy family environment, by all appearances the Gibsons made the best of their lot until things took an unexpected turn for the worst: several years after the divorce, Inez's mother wanted to take her back, and informed her adoptive parents that she was coming to do just that. At first it might seem that Inez would be overjoyed by such news, but in fact the effect of her mother's letter was quite the opposite: Inez declared that she would rather die than go back to live with her own mother, and that is exactly what happened on December 21st 1900, when she was found hanging by the neck in her bedroom closet by her younger brother, Otto, as detailed in this extract from *A Brief History of Malvern* by author John D. Paddock, which was printed in 1917 in the town newspaper, *The*

Malvern Leader [I have made no changes to the grammar or spelling]*:*

The startling topic and casuality of the afternoon has been the death of little Inez Gibson at the home of her foster parents, Mr and Mrs T.D. Gibson, and the tragic manner of the little one's death. The brother Otto and Inez had been playing upon the porch and lawn below when Inez, tiring of the play, wanted Otto to go with her up stairs to the playroom, and she run up the stairs, but the brother remained below just a little while when he too climbed the stairs, and was dazed and horrified to find his little sister hanging in the open closet from the room with the jumping rope about her neck. He worked frantically to take her down, but unable to do so rushed to his uncle and aunt at the store. Mr. Gibson quickly reached the scene, and placed the little form upon her bed, and when doctors Scott and Love arrived every effort possible was made to bring too the life, but it was of no avail, it had gone. There could be no verdict rendered but accidental death [author's emphasis added]. The deepest sympathy of the whole community goes out to Mr. and Mrs. Gibson in this sad and tragic bereavement that has come to them. The funeral service at the home by Reverend H.P. McDowell and the little casket that is covered with beautiful flowers is taken to place of burial.

Let's take a look at the claims made by the newspaper article a little more closely. The phrase that jumps out most to this author is: *There could be no verdict rendered but accidental death.* This single sentence is nothing short of ridiculous. We are expected to believe that the most likely reason for a depressed 12 year-old girl to be found hanging in her own closet with a jump-rope around her neck is a tragic accident – in other words, pure happenstance. What of the possibility – I would actually go so far as to say the *probability* – that Inez was so upset at the prospect of being forced to leave the only real family she had ever known and be dragged away by a mother who had already abandoned her once, that she took her own life rather than submit to such a fate?

Why would Inez have been playing with her jump rope in a closet, of all places, rather than in the more spacious playing room itself, or out on the lawn where there was more room to swing the rope? And how exactly did the rope manage to get entangled around both the child's neck and some form of rigid structure inside the closet, such as a shelf or stanchion, to such a degree that Inez was unable to escape, and therefore accidentally hanged herself?

Yet suicide was generally seen as an utterly shameful thing in 1900, and the idea that a child might contemplate it, let alone actually go through with it, would have been truly shocking. Far better for all concerned if the official story claimed that the entire affair had been a terrible accident, a one-in-a-million fluke that had ended tragically... It is not difficult to see how the physicians filling out Inez's death certificate might choose to frame this tragedy in such a way as to allow the Gibsons to believe that their adopted daughter had not committed such an act. I cannot say that I would blame them in the slightest.

The truth about whether Inez took her own life or died as the result of a freak accident will almost certainly never be known for sure.

Yet the *Leader* article is very clear about the fact that poor Inez died at home, not – as a number of sources have erroneously stated – in what has come to be known as

"Inez's Room" at Malvern Manor. With that being the case, why would she then haunt the Manor in the first place, especially a closet that she had never been near, let alone been found hanging in?

Having discussed the matter with Josh, my companions and I came up with several possible answers to that question.

The possibility that I consider to be the least likely was that Inez Gibson, or some part of her consciousness at least, really does haunt Malvern Manor to this day, though certainly that would not be unprecedented. At the time of writing, she died 118 years ago; in the literature of paranormal research, there are many documented and well-attested instances of spirits lingering at a given location for that length of time, and sometimes much longer. It is not inconceivable that the supposed spirit of this poor unfortunate girl could be exactly what she appears to be.

Why, then, would she haunt Malvern Manor, rather than the private residence in which she died? Josh believes that the house no longer stands, saying that it is now just a vacant lot. Some researchers have theorized that certain locations are the equivalent of lighthouses or beacons for spirits, a place that they are drawn to in order to congregate and be in like-minded company. Some take this theory further still, and propose that these are places at which spirit entities can travel back and forth between this plane of existence and the next via 'doorways' that are referred to as portals. This would be the classic, long-term haunted house, which seems to remain paranormally active for generations.

Could Malvern Manor be just such a place, and if so, could Inez's spirit have been attracted to the hotel when she passed on?

Things get a little more perplexing when we follow this line of enquiry much further, however. The story of Inez having been supposedly found hanging in the closet up on the second floor has been proven to be untrue, yet it is one that has been propagated far and wide, and has now become something of an urban legend. It is important to point out that this was by no means a case of intentional deception on the part of the owners or visiting paranormal investigators; before they hired a private investigator to conduct background research into the building and its colorful history, they simply took the story at face value.

In an interview with *The Daily Nonpareil's* Mike Brownlee for a February 14, 2017 titled "*Do ghosts roam Malvern Manor? Haunt offers frights, questions to visitors,*"

Malvern Manor co-owner Kurt Fricke addressed the story of Inez.

> *One ghost who supposedly lives in the home is Inez Gibson, a 12-year-old girl found dead in a closet hanging from a jump rope in 1901. [Inez actually passed in 1900 – R.E.] On the tour, Fricke pointed out what they call "Inez's room," where they've heard her name on recordings.*
> *"My daughter asked the ghost how old she was. She said '12.'"*

The wording of the article does not explicitly state that Inez died in that specific closet, just that her name has been recorded in there. As detailed elsewhere in this book, my friends from AAPI recorded some extraordinary SLS camera footage in that same closet during their first visit to Malvern Manor in 2017. Since it was discovered that Inez died off-site, Josh and his colleagues make a point of telling visitors that Inez Gibson probably never stepped foot in Malvern Manor at all, let alone in what will probably always be called "Inez's room."

The constant stream of visiting paranormal

investigators and para-tourists raises another intriguing potential explanation for the numerous EVPs and other ITC communications that purport to come from Inez.

"You guys got the name 'Inez' last time you were here, right?" Josh asked Stephen, Erik, and Jill.

"Multiple times, through the Geoport," Stephen confirmed, referring to a device which, some people claim, allows spirit entities to reorder certain snippets of dialog into intelligible English phrases in order for them to communicate with the living.

"So you have to wonder," Josh went on, "Did we manifest a ghost...in other words, did we create one? Speak it into existence, if you will."

"You related the story of Inez to us on our first day here," Erik pointed out, "and then the very next day, we started to get that name appearing on our audio equipment. Then there was what looked like the hanging kid's body in the closet that we got on the SLS camera in Inez's room."

Jill said that it was almost as if somebody was putting on a show for them, one that matched the narrative of Inez's death and subsequent haunting of the room that was named after her.

There is a fairly well-known concept in paranormal

circles known as the thought form. The thought form is a commonly-held belief among many cultures from around the world, and has different names: for example, Tibetans refer to it as the *tulpa*.

A thought form is essentially an artificially-manufactured entity – it is not manufactured by technology, but rather by deliberate effort on the part of one or more human beings. If one puts enough time, effort, and sheer willpower into the task, it appears to be possible to generate a completely independent extra-corporeal being. Perhaps the best-known example is the infamous "Philip Experiment," which took place in Toronto in 1972. A team of researchers intentionally created an entity which they named Philip, going into great detail in outlining his backstory and personal character traits in much the same way as role-playing gamers might create the back-story for a character in *Dungeons and Dragons* or *Pathfinder*. Lo and behold, it wasn't long before Philip – or something calling itself Philip, at any rate – began to manifest, answering questions that were posed to it with answers that were completely consistent with its pre-created back-story. The Philip Experiment was not without its detractors, many of whom dismiss the entire thing as a case of overactive subconscious minds on the part of the participants, yet the research group reported numerous instances of physical phenomena such as a table lifting itself off the ground without human intervention, unexplained cold spots and various auditory phenomena. It seems that whatever truly did take place during the Philip Experiment, it somehow managed to interact physically with the material world around it.

Now fast-forward to the last few years at Malvern Manor. Inez's story, most specifically the part about her untimely death and subsequent 'afterlife,' has been repeated over and over again innumerable times to those who have come to visit. Is it possible that all of the directed mental energy that was put into that common narrative over that period of time has created a thought form that is somewhat akin to Philip – a psychic 'blank slate' of an entity that has now taken on the persona of a child who died tragically in 1900?

That would go some way toward explaining why the voice of a young girl calling itself Inez has been heard in the vicinity of a room where the real Inez almost certainly never set foot. The Inez who currently interacts with paranormal investigators at Malvern Manor could quite possibly be nothing more than a soulless energy construct, a product of the hopes, thoughts, and expectations of hundreds (if not thousands) of people who have come to Malvern Manor and heard her story told.

There is another alternative explanation, however, and this one is far more sinister and disturbing than the two that have already been mentioned. Many seasoned paranormal investigators will tell you that some of the darker, more malevolent spirit entities (I am deliberately not going to use the word *demonic*, as I think it's massively over-used) will often try to pass themselves off as being the polar opposite of what they actually are – in other words, they will come across as being innocent, vulnerable children.

In other words, exactly as Malvern Manor's version of Inez presents itself...

As we have already seen, many people have spoken of there being a malign force of some kind at the heart of the Malvern Manor haunting. While some have theorized that this may be the ghost of Captain Cullers, in this investigator's view, he seems to be an unlikely candidate. As Josh pointed out during our interview, while the Captain is indeed an active haunter at the Manor, he tends to be more of the disgruntled, cantankerous type, rather than being a malevolent one.

"I don't think he appreciates what we're doing here at all with this ghost-hunting stuff," Josh said, "Which is probably why he's been known to push and shove people up on the second floor from time to time."

So the Captain doesn't like the intrusive, potentially disrespectful behavior of the paranormal teams that regularly visit what he still sees as being his domain. I can understand that, and to be honest, I can relate to it. Look at it from his perspective. Who would appreciate a near-constant parade of strangers stampeding through the house, demanding that you move something on cue or answer their questions, no matter how ridiculous or outlandish? It would be enough to try the patience of a saint.

But there are no indications that the ghost of Captain Cullers has ever done anything approaching real harm to anybody – shoves and minor scratches seem to be the extent of his expressions of anger. By all accounts, there appears to be something else haunting the second floor; a something that is both territorial and a good deal less friendly than the good Captain.

We discussed the possibility that this force, entity,

call it what you will, may sometimes choose to pass itself off as being the spirit of Inez for its own murky purposes. The sound of children running playing has been heard up on the second floor by multiple visitors to Malvern Manor, and a number of EVPs that sound uncannily like the voice of a little girl have been recorded up there, some of them clearly saying the name Inez.

Is it more likely that the spirit of Inez still walks at Malvern Manor, that a kind of thought form has been created based around the story of her death, or that something else is masquerading as her? In the end, it all comes down to a matter of personal opinion, but we resolved to spend a lot of time upstairs over the coming days in an attempt to shed some light on this particular mystery.

"It's interesting to me that we have something that sounds like a little girl; acts like a little girl; calls you by name, and asks you to come and play with her..." Josh said thoughtfully. "It's changed my thought process, because now I'm thinking that maybe this is something that's trying to f*** with us. Something that's dark.

"Right after I first became involved with the Manor, we started getting EVPs of a little girl upstairs in that room. We've gotten that specific name – Inez – since the very beginning. Although we used to think that Inez died here, now we're pretty sure that her home was about two blocks away and is now just an empty lot. Still, two blocks is fairly close, right? So we didn't really question the identity of the spirit that was giving us those EVPs at first."

"When we were here last October, we asked Inez what her favorite color was, and the response was pink," Erik said. "We promised we'd get her something in that color when we came back. So we bought her a pink Easter basket. It's full of pink stuff too."

"Aww, how sweet." Josh seemed genuinely touched. Then Erik ruined the moment by saying that they'd done it in case Inez got angry and pinned one of them to the ceiling. Good old Erik, ever the pragmatist...

Josh mentioned that the building that is now known as Malvern Manor was once the social center of the town, playing host to weddings, some funerals (though not, we believe, that of Inez) and many other community functions.

"This place was hopping all the time," he concluded. "That's a *lot* of potential energy."

Chapter Four
A Haunted History

Furiously taking notes, I asked Josh about some of the other strange happenings that were reported at the Manor. One was the now-infamous Shadow Man, Josh said, citing the time that seasoned paranormal investigator Johnny Houser was standing in the nursing wing and turned to find a large black shadowy mass rushing toward him, only to disappear into thin air just inches from his face.

"Don't ask me why, but for some reason people have been reporting seeing a lot of smaller shadow figures lately. Child-sized, and even toddler-sized, ducking in and out of rooms and moving very fast. One of the very first people to catch sight of one was Dustin Pari (of *Ghost Hunters International*) and ever since that night, which was about a year ago, more and more very similar claims have begun pouring in. They're all reporting the same thing, and it seems to be behaving in the same way."

"We first came here about a year ago, a couple of weeks after Dustin visited," Jill pointed out, "and that was one of the things that we saw. Tiny black shadow figures."

"We've also gotten claims of something crawling along the ceiling," Josh added, "although what the hell that is, I have no idea. I've never encountered anything like that myself."

That brought to mind the so-called 'Creeper' at Waverly Hills Sanatorium in Louisville, Kentucky. Ostensibly one of the most haunted places in the world (though my own night there was very quiet indeed) many visitors to the sanatorium have reported seeing a shadowy figure which has somewhat human-like proportions, crawling along the upper walls and ceilings. Were we dealing with a very specific subset of the shadow figure phenomenon in both cases? I found the possibility intriguing.

"I'd suggest that whatever is in the attic is pretty dark and nasty," Josh went on. "For the last three days, the attic has been very active, according to the people who have been up there."

We made a note to spend some time up in the attic during the course of our investigation. "I've got to ask you, Josh, in your opinion...why do you think that Malvern Manor is so paranormally active?"

It was a question that had been bugging me ever since I'd learned of the existence of the place and its reputation for being extremely haunted. To the very best of our knowledge, it wasn't built on a battlefield or a burial site; there had been little in the way of death there, apart from the usual number of perfectly natural deaths that would be expected of any care home for senior citizens.

Josh took a deep breath. I was half-expecting a sales pitch of some kind, but to his credit he said, "I frankly can't say for sure. A lot of the weird stuff that takes place here seems to be psychological in nature...cat and mouse bullshit. One part of the building will start acting up, and when you go over there to investigate, something strange will start happening elsewhere. It's almost as if whatever haunts this place wants to give investigators the run-around.

"If I had to make an educated guess, I'd say that much of it has to do with the clientele who lived here at Malvern Manor during the later part of its life."

"You're talking about the fact that some of them had mental health or addiction issues?" I asked.

"That's exactly right."

We were entering delicate territory now. The subject of mental health care is a very sensitive and contentious one. One thing that cannot be denied, however, is that we as a society have not done very well in taking care of the mentally unwell and disabled during the past. When I was conducting research for my book, *The World's Most Haunted Hospitals,* I discovered that while many regular, everyday hospitals and medical centers have their ghosts, by far the most active tended to be those facilities that were once known as "lunatic asylums." While they were intended to care for the mentally ill, many such asylums paid lip-service to the idea of delivering care, and instead became places where society's castoffs and lost souls could be incarcerated, out of sight and out of mind.

Fortunately, this was not such a place. When it was operating as the Nishna Cottage Nursing Home, the Manor was actually said to be a place of great warmth and friendliness, one which had a very familial feel to it. By all accounts, the residents of the nursing home were well-treated and cared for by the staff and owners, who understood that for some of the unfortunate people who were entrusted into their care, this was the only kind of home and family that they would ever know.

A local newspaper article dating back to June 14, 1956, titled *"Piper Hotel to be Changed to Modern Rest Home Here"* tells of the building's transition from hotel to nursing home:

One of Malvern's earliest business institutions will be discontinued shortly, according to an announcement this week by Mrs. Cuba Cox, proprietor of the Piper Hotel.

The hotel has been sold to three ladies, Mrs. Bessie Smith and Mrs. Mildred Peterson of Red Oak and Mrs.Eyvonne Wederquist of Glenwood, who will remodel the building and convert it into a rest home. The hotel, formerly the Cottage, was established in the 1880s and long has been a prominent institution in the community. It was modernized some 18 years ago by the late R.K. Piper and generally enjoyed good patronage. Its sale will leave the community without a hostelry.

The transaction was completed Thursday morning so complete plans for the new enterprise were not available. Mrs. Smith stated that the building had been inspected and given a satisfactory report by the state fire marshal and that it will be operated under the provisions for such established by the state board of health.

While the number of patients it can care for

has not been determined, the new owners believe
they will be handled to accept around 45.

So, why did the nursing home close down?

According to Josh, an inspection by representatives of the state of Iowa determined that none of the corridors were wide enough to accommodate a moving hospital bed, which was one of the requirements to operate such a facility. The state therefore pulled the owners' license to run a nursing home, and the patients were duly sent elsewhere. The building changed its designation, becoming a residential care facility, which meant that those who lived inside its walls were people with chronic problems in need of long-term care; most were afflicted with mental illness in one of its many shapes and forms, whereas others suffered from any number of various addictions and disorders. One shudders to think what would have happened to these unfortunate souls if Malvern's residential care facility hadn't been there to act as a lifeline.

In a newspaper article dating back to April 28, 1994, the capacity of the Nishna Cottage privately-owned care facility is stated as 35, ten less than the number of patients accepted by the nursing home. The article goes on to say that the facility serves "*those who are mentally and physically challenged, as well as the chemically dependent, serving a six county area in southwest Iowa, northwest Missouri, and southeast Nebraska*" and, "*They endeavor to teach the necessary skills to function independently, as in personal hygiene, house-keeping skills, maintaining a routine as well as a time schedule. Their primary goal is to restore the clients' self-esteem and human dignity.*"

The staff and owner (a Mrs. Reid) all deserve a great deal of credit for taking care of the special needs population for six entire counties, including those recovering from drug addiction and alcoholism. Such work is usually difficult, sometimes dangerous, usually goes unheralded, and yet is absolutely essential, and this author's hat goes off to them for doing it for so many years.

"I've got a lot of respect for her," Josh said. "She was by all accounts a very big-hearted person, one who just wanted to help everybody...the sort of lady who would go out into the street to check on a passer-by, making sure that they had somewhere to eat and a roof over their head."

Mrs. Reid ran her residential facility until 2005, when it was taken over by another buyer. When the structure failed to meet the stringent requirements outlined by the fire marshal, it finally closed down for good shortly afterward.

A piercing scream suddenly came from somewhere directly above us. We were all a little startled, with the exception of Josh, who cocked a nonchalant thumb toward the ceiling and said, "Tour group.

"Another weird thing," he went on, coming back to the subject of the building itself, "is the number of former owners that have died under strange circumstances, mostly in the early days of its life. It was going through owners like they were losing in a card game. There was constant turnover. As a co-owner, I try to watch my back as much as possible.

"One guy was leaving here at the end of a workday, and walked out that front door right there" – he pointed toward the main entrance – "and got two or three steps, then just dropped dead on the spot right outside the building on the sidewalk there. Massive heart attack, aneurysm, whatever, I don't know, but he was stone cold dead before he hit the ground.

"Then there was the guy who was working on a piece of farm equipment at home. The thing literally exploded and blasted pieces of this poor guy all over the place."

"I hate to use a loaded word, Josh, but is this place cursed?" I didn't believe in such things personally, but some people did.

"I freakin' hope not," he shuddered. "I really do. But I just plain don't know."

Just then, the tour group stomped down the stairs and headed for the front door.

"How was it?" Josh asked the last one out. "Sounded as though you got the shit scared out of you."

The female tourist, slightly wide-eyed and looking a little jittery, answered that yes, they'd gotten a little frightened up in the attic, mostly because there were scratching sounds coming from all around them up there. As we would later discover, this was most likely caused by the tree branches scraping against the roof and the side of the building. There was nothing even remotely paranormal about it. People in the attic do sometimes hear a different kind of scratching, however, coming from one of the corners; in those cases, it is obviously happening inside the room, and is said by those who hear it to be quite different from the sound made by the trees.

"Are you guys staying?" the tourist asked us. "I was

antagonizing whatever was up there, so...sorry, I guess. I probably woke it up."

Before I could ask her what *it* was, she was gone, dashing off to catch up with the rest of her group. The front door slammed shut behind them. Josh locked it from the inside.

"Okay guys, how would you like a tour?"

He led us into what had once been the parlor or lobby, a large front room which had black plastic covering all the windows. I recognized it immediately as the room in which Katrina Weidman had spent a night during the *Paranormal Lockdown* episode. In fact, there was the green leather recliner that she'd said was really comfortable. Later on I would put that theory to the test, and had to agree – it really was a comfy chair.

Two wheelchairs stood a few feet apart on either side of the room. Tape had been used to mark the position of their wheels. I asked Josh if they were original to the facility.

"They are," he confirmed, pointing at one of the chairs, "and *that* one has a serious reputation for being haunted. In fact just the other week, it chased a tour group out of here all by itself. They were pretty freaked out. They chair both like to move on their own, so that's why we mark their position with tape. The older wheelchair seems to have a mind of its own, and it's definitely the more active of the two."

I took a closer look. It was just an old wheelchair. It didn't have any sort of bad vibe about it (not that I'm very sensitive where such things are concerned) but when I was leafing through the visitor's book later on during our stay, I found a number of intriguing entries concerning it. Most backed up what Josh was telling us, accounts of the wheelchair moving of its own volition, but one entry was a little more disturbing than that. Its author claims to have caught sight of the apparition of an old man named Harry sitting in that wheelchair, going so far as to draw a sketch of him in the guest book.

Josh confirmed that Harry had been a real resident of the care facility. When he had been given a guided tour of the place by the former staff members shortly after buying the place, they had told him that Harry had been mostly confined to that particular wheelchair. He had rarely spoken to others, instead keeping himself mostly to himself, and the parlor was his favorite room. If he couldn't be in the parlor, then he liked to be outside on the deck, enjoying a little sunshine if the weather was nice.

Harry kept a little transistor radio pressed to his hear, and liked to hum and whistle along with whatever tune happened to be playing. This probably explains why a number of visitors to Malvern Manor have heard (and sometimes even recorded) the sound of disembodied whistling and humming coming from the empty parlor.

"This place stared out as a hotel in the late 1800s," Josh went on. "This room – the parlor – has probably been the most general-purpose, down through the years. This is where people would check in and get their rooms, for example."

"Malvern's a fairly small town," I pointed out. "Was there a lot of business for a hotel this side?"

"More than you'd think. It was built to capitalize on the railroad that came through Malvern. A lot of travelers spent time under this roof." Josh pointed to a large framed photo portrait hanging on the wall. It showed a rather severe-looking man. I recognized him as Captain Cullers. "One of the earliest owners was this man, who we like to call the Captain. He raised a family here in town, and had strong ties with Malvern in general and this building in particular. Maybe that's why he doesn't appear to have left. A lot of visitors claim to have run into him up on the second floor. In fact, we've even named a part of it "The Captain's Corner" and the room it leads to is known as "The Captain's Room."

I studied the picture for a few moments. The Captain was mostly bald, with a long grey beard. His expression was a little on the stoic side, although that wasn't particularly unusual considering that the photograph had been taken in the 1800s, when long exposure times meant that subjects couldn't crack a smile while they were getting their picture taken.

Curious, I asked Josh about the owners' long-term plans for the place. He replied that they wanted to put as much money as possible into renovating the structure of Malvern Manor, while at the same time leaving the guts of the building – its rooms and corridors – relatively untouched. It certainly sounded like a great idea to me. The place already attracts more than its fair share of ghost hunters, and the idea of preserving it so that many more could experience the place was very appealing.

Chapter Five
Gracie and the Shadow Man

Staying on the ground floor, Josh led us down a long
hallway, passing open doors on both sides. He finally
stopped at a room about halfway down on the left. I
recognized it instantly: this had been Gracie's room.

"The jury's still out on all of this," Josh said, leaning
back against the doorframe, "but I think it's possible that
some of the so-called 'spirits' we encounter here are actually
the alternate personalities of a lady that was called 'Grace' or
'Gracie.'"

I'd heard of Gracie while doing my research on
Malvern Manor. Hers seemed to be a particularly sad case.
Diagnosed with Multiple Personality Disorder, she was
known to transition from one personality to another in rapid
succession. One day, nurses who sat with Grace documented
at least thirteen distinct personalities over the course of just
two hours. Coming in both male and female variants, some
of those personas must have been downright chilling – such
as the gruff male voice that would insist that "*The Devil's
coming to get me,*" over and over again. So convincing were
the vocal changes that sometimes the staff would think that a

man had snuck into Grace's room and was talking to her. Small wonder, then, that Grace's room on the ground floor is reputed to be one of the most haunted parts of the Manor.

Josh had raised an intriguing point. If some part of the human personality does indeed survive bodily death, as many people believe, then in the case of patients who suffer from schizophrenia and Multiple Personality Disorder, as Gracie did, would those separate and distinct personalities all survive too, in some form? In other words, if Grace had thirteen personalities, could each of them potentially haunt Malvern Manor to the present day, being mistaken by paranormal investigators for thirteen entirely different entities? It was something I had never considered before, and I found the possibility to be a fascinating one.

Appropriately enough, this condition goes by many names. In addition to Multiple Personality Disorder (MPD), it is also often referred to informally as Split Personality Disorder. Some behavioral health clinicians prefer the term Dissociative Identity Disorder (DID). It is a condition which still baffles doctors today.

Consider the recently-publicized case of Kim Noble, who has over 20 documented personalities. Although she has one dominant personality named Patricia, Kim has a tendency to switch seamlessly between any number of alternate personalities in the blink of eye. They include a little boy who writes fluent Latin, a single mother who craves romantic companionship, and a 12 year-old girl named Ria that frequently draws pictures of children being beaten and abused.

MPD is as fascinating as it is heartbreaking. Behavioral specialists have pointed out that the condition seems to manifest shortly after the patient experiences some kind of severe emotional trauma. The mind seems to 'fracture,' for want of a better word, breaking itself up into multiple independent compartments. This seems to act as a defense mechanism of some kind, helping the sufferer deal with the after-effects of whatever traumatic condition caused the personality split. Most of the time, the various personalities have at least some sense of mutual awareness. They will often jockey for control of the patient's body, getting themselves embroiled in a kind of multi-personality tug of war.

The room was fairly dark, thanks to the window being covered. Apart from a bed and a wheelchair (both of which were original), there was little else in the room apart from a small selection of toys and a pair of ladies' spectacles on a shelf.

I resolved to spend at least a few hours investigating Gracie's Room. Maybe she – or one of her alternate personalities – would make her presence known.

The nursing home wing, added on in 1956, may not have seen an actual patient for years, but little reminders of their presence can be found everywhere. Turning left at the nurse's station, Josh led us to the end of what he called "The Shadow Man's hallway." The door at the end of the hallway was covered with a hanging blanket. Immediately to the right of that was the door to Room 2, which was securely padlocked. It was being used for private storage, and regrettably we would have no access to it.

"More than once a black, shadowy figure has been seen coming out of the doorway of Room 2, without opening the door first," Josh explained. "It turns and likes to run right at the people who see it. They're usually standing right about where we are now. As I said earlier, we've come to call it the Shadow Man."

He went on to say that although he uses the term *running*, the motion itself is very different to that of a living person running; the Shadow Man covers half the length of the hallway in less than a second, something which would clearly be impossible for a flesh and blood human being. Those who have been on the receiving end of this rather intimidating brush with the paranormal find it, quite understandably, to be very unnerving.

Sounding a little rueful, Josh told us that this particular experience had sent more than a few visitors fleeing Malvern Manor as fast as their legs could carry them – himself included, on one occasion.

"In all my time here, I've experienced this three times," he went on. "The first two times, I was shocked – taken completely by surprise. The last time, I had to stand there for two solid hours, practically begging the Shadow Man to come out and play."

"And he did?" I asked.

"Oh, hell yes. Unfortunately, even though I'd been hoping that he would come out and rush me again, it still took me by surprise when it finally happened. I'm a little embarrassed to say that I flinched again, and he disappeared right in front of my face."

"Did you feel anything at the time?" I was expecting him to say that he had felt a blast of freezing cold air or an electro-static tingling sensation.

"I felt a sense of complete dread and fear. Just as

soon as he hits you, the feeling's gone. It's really weird."

It is very telling that the Shadow Man 'assault' happens the same way each and every time; it never varies. I ventured the opinion that this sounded more like a case of a residual haunting to me rather than one of the intelligent variety. Josh nodded his head in agreement, and added that so far, his attempts to identify a specific time of day, day of the week, week of the year, or even phase of the moon during which the Shadow Man appeared had so far been a failure. The phenomenon was occurring at seemingly random intervals, without any apparent rhyme or reason behind it other than the presence of intruders in the Shadow Man's hallway.

"The day after the *Paranormal Lockdown* episode aired, a former employee reached out to me and said than in Room 2, there used to be a patient who was 6'7" tall, non-verbal, and completely deranged. Supposedly he had killed two people in the past. The staff were said to be so scared of him that they wouldn't even assist him with putting on his shoes in the morning."

We found this particular revelation to be nothing less than shocking. Assuming that the former employee was telling the truth (something of which there was no guarantee), just how did somebody with a homicidal past end up in a non-secure facility such as this, as opposed to one of the bigger, more secure state-run facilities that were far better equipped to cope with violent patients?

"This gentleman's claim to fame was that whenever the nurses were doing bed checks – which was usually on the hour, every hour – he would come out of his room and chase whoever had been sent to check on him. I find the parallel between his behavior and that of the Shadow Man to be fascinating. It sounds a lot like we could be dealing with the same guy."

Frankly, if I'd been faced with the same situation as those poor nurses, I would probably have been alarmed too. As a paramedic, I'm sometimes faced with similarly aggressive patients. They can be extremely unpredictable, often violently so, and the only truly safe and humane way to deal with that kind of behavior is to sedate and then physically restrain them for their own good. The thought of standing nose-to-nose with a belligerent psychiatric patient who has just charged at me, makes my blood run cold.

Once again, assuming that the story about the homicidal patient having once occupied Room 2 is correct, then this really does seem like a good candidate for the identity of the Shadow Man. Despite the aggressive behavior exhibited by the Shadow Man, however, it must be pointed out that none of the investigators who have encountered him have gotten scratched, shoved, hit, or otherwise physically harmed...

...with one exception.

"When they put Johnny Houser's ass back there, he did get touched and grabbed a few times – this happened just last week. You know, I was hanging out beneath the car port at about four-thirty in the afternoon back when Johnny had his big run-in with the Shadow Man. He's a big guy and a real badass, but let me tell you, he was out the back door like lightning when that happened to him."

We were suddenly distracted when Stephen saw a shadow flit across the doorway of Room 3. As soon as he looked more closely, it had gone. A trick of the light, I wondered, or were things starting to get going?

"Now, this room also has quite the story." Josh led us to the opposite end of the hallway. We filed into Room 7. It looked spartan and grimy, like most of the other patient rooms. "This door has been opening and closing all by itself lately."

"What's with the random kid's shoe?" Erik wanted to

know, pointing to a single lonely-looking child's sneaker that was sitting on top of a water pipe.

"Hell if I know," Josh shrugged, "but they're all over the Manor. I don't know if visitors are bringing them in and moving them around or if the ghosts are."

He was absolutely right; as we went around the building that week, we found several of the little shoes, in all different styles and sizes. Some were placed on top of wardrobes; others were hidden in closets and drawers. It seemed an odd thing to find, considering that this really wasn't a place for children.

"People keep reporting the smell of body odor turning up unexpectedly in this room," Josh went on, continuing the story of Room 7. "It's not just unwashed visitors, before you ask. It comes and it goes at random, from what we can tell. A lot of female visitors – and they're almost *always* female for some reason, never men – tend to get their ankles grabbed in here too..."

Chapter Six
Up to the Second

There was a lot for us to think about as we retraced our steps back into the main part of the building and followed Josh upstairs to the second floor. As we approached the section of hallway known as "The Captain's Corner," he pointed out a series of smeared bloodstains running along the wall. Nobody is really sure what caused them.

In addition to this specific stretch of the corridor, Josh told us that the Captain seemed to be particularly active in Room 24. Visiting investigators had been struck on the arms and legs, hard enough to raise bruises. The Captain may not have built the hotel which would become Malvern Manor, but he did run the place, and casts a long shadow over it to this day. Josh has no doubt that the Captain disapproves of the droves of paranormal investigators and ghost-hunters who flock there each year, and is apparently not at all shy about making his displeasure known.

Our next stop was Suzie's room. Not long after assuming co-ownership of the building, Josh noticed that the name 'Suzie' was appearing on more and more EVP recordings and coming through spirit boxes that were used in this room. When he spoke to a number of people who had worked there in the past, he was gratified to find the name was validated by them.

Josh made it clear that the former nurses who had spoken with him could only tell him certain things about Suzie, as they were still bound by the laws governing medical privacy. Although middle-aged in terms of her physical body, Suzie was said to have had a mental age of approximately eight or nine years old. A few children's coloring books were discovered in Suzie's room, which is presumably something which brought her great joy; subsequent visitors have added to that collection, bringing in more coloring books, crayons, pens, and toys for Suzie to play with. It was a touching gesture, one that showed the more compassionate side of people who came to visit the Manor, and I found it to be rather heartwarming.

During their first visit, Jill had been coloring in one of the books left on Suzie's bed and had asked the question, "What's your favorite color?" She was rewarded with a Class A EVP (the clearest quality obtainable) which distinctly said the word, Pink. Jill promised to bring Suzie something pink when she returned, and true to her word, she had brought a pink Easter basket full of goodies along with her this time.

It is believed that Suzie is somehow confined to this room. Her voice doesn't seem to crop up on audio devices anywhere else around the building, and more ominously, the phrases *Scared* and *He won't let me* have been recorded by investigators who have asked why she wouldn't go outside. One has to wonder exactly who *'he'* is – the Captain, perhaps, or somebody else?

Further down the hall on the right was one of the main attractions so far as we were concerned – Inez's room. From day one, Josh and his colleagues picked up activity in this room which seemed to come from the little girl who called herself by that name...assuming that it really *was* a little girl.

"Most of the activity I've experienced back here is hearing the running of her footsteps up and down the hallway outside," Josh told us. "It's definitely the sound of a kid. I have two small daughters at home, and trust me: I *know* that sound."

We all laughed.

"You hear her giggling, and sometimes she'll call out your name and ask you to come and play with her. Knowing what we know now about Inez not actually dying here at Malvern Manor, I'm not sure exactly what this spirit really is

– whether it truly is a child, or whether it's something else. But what I can say is that Inez roams wherever she wants to be. We've run into her up in the attic, downstairs, over on the nursing home wing, you name it. She goes wherever she wants.

Inez's room was pretty nondescript, with a window, a closet, a very old TV, and a host of kid's toys. On their first visit to Malvern Manor, AAPI had shot a fascinating piece of SLS video footage in that closet which had looked eerily like a child-sized figure hanging by the neck, while a second smaller figure tried to pull it down to the ground.

The atmosphere was calm and peaceful in Inez's room right now. I hoped that things might change as the night went on.

Wandering back the way we had come and heading in the general direction of the attic, Josh told us that Malvern Manor had suffered four known fires during the course of its lifetime. The only traces left of them were visible in the attic, where the rafters still bore the black marks of charring. We would go up there later.

Crossing the landing at the top of the main staircase, we now found ourselves in a separate second floor wing, one which paralleled Gracie's room and the long corridor leading down to the nursing wing, both of which were now directly beneath us.

We made our way to Hank's room (or Henry's room, depending on whichever name the entity that haunts it likes to be called on any given day) which is number 15. "He's the stereotypical grumpy old man," Josh explained, "and we're told that during his lifetime, he liked nothing more than to sit out on the front porch and throw rocks at children."

I couldn't help but smile at that. I was starting to like Hank already.

"You mess with these at your peril," he went on, sliding open the top drawer of a wooden dresser. We peered inside. Several items of clothing were stacked in there, including shirts, socks, and even underwear, which supposedly belonged to Hank. "He really hates it when anybody messes with his stuff. Particularly women, for some reason; Hank really doesn't appreciate having ladies in his room."

Connie, Susan, and Jill shared a look. Unless I missed my guess, Hank was going to have his work cut out for him if he wanted to try and intimidate these three.

"What size are they?" I wanted to know. Stephen picked one of the shirts up and checked the label.

"Large. I'm gonna put this on, sit out on the front porch, and throw rocks at passing kids."

Fortunately for us, he was joking...I think.

In the past, putting on an article of Hank's clothing had caused the sound of a disembodied male voice to begin yelling from one of the empty corners of the room. It was a theory that I couldn't wait to put to the test.

Moving a little further on down the hallway, we came to a pair of rooms which faced one another. The story associated with Rooms 17 and 18 was a disturbing and unsettling one, and it must be pointed out that there is absolutely no conclusive proof that it ever truly happened. Josh told us that the source of information behind this story was, once again, a former member of staff.

According to this informant, the male resident who occupied Room 18 had made a careful note of the bed check schedule, so that he knew precisely when the staff members would make their rounds and look in on their charges to make sure that all was well. Once the check had been completed, he was said to sneak across the hallway into Room 17, where he would sexually assault the man who resided there. This abhorrent scenario was supposedly played out several times each week, and if it is true, one can only imagine the untold misery and suffering experienced by the poor victim.

One is forced to wonder whether the staff knew about the illicit, forced sexual activity which was going on right underneath their noses. I would like to think that if they had, they would have dealt with the situation immediately. Yet as things turned out, there may have been more to the story than meets the eye.

Prior to our own visit, Dustin Pari had conducted his own investigation at Malvern Manor. Dustin, Josh, and some fellow investigators were conducting EVP burst sessions in Room 17. Quite understandably, they had wanted to know about the truth (or lack thereof) of the stories surrounding the alleged sexual assault.

When the burst recordings were played back, those present were surprised to find out that their questions had most definitely been answered.

"That never happened," boomed a man's indignant voice, an unmistakable Class A EVP.

They leapt on the opportunity to ask what actually had happened.

"I loved him."

The investigators looked at one another, open-mouthed. Was it possible that what had been reported as a string of sexual assaults was in fact totally consensual? Josh certainly seemed to think so. He went on to describe a marathon two hour back-and-forth EVP session (most run for only a fraction of that time) in which a coherent narrative began to emerge: if the disembodied voices were to be believed, then the two men occupying rooms 17 and 18 were actually a couple, and simply engaged in the type of activity that most loving couples do.

To venture any further down this road would open up quite the can of worms. For starters, specific details about these residents would be protected by confidentiality rules and healthcare privacy legislation. It would also be grossly unfair to accuse any staff members of failing to monitor their charges properly. One might also conjecture that if the two men were indeed romantically involved, the staff may easily have turned a blind eye to their activities, seeing them as being relatively harmless.

The truth is that although EVP sessions such as that led by Dustin and Josh have cast some interesting new light on the story of rooms 17 and 18, we will never truly know for sure either way – this is another of the many mysteries associated with Malvern Manor.

Chapter Seven
The Attic

We had certainly been given plenty of food for thought. Walking to the very end of the hallway, Josh unlatched a wooden door off to the left and stuck his head inside.

"Sarah, are you still up there?"

"No, not at all," a female voice deadpanned. Josh chuckled.

"Come on up to the attic. Sarah's spending some time up there on her own. She really loves this place."

He disappeared through the doorway. One by one, we followed him inside, and made our way carefully up a narrow staircase into the attic. There we found Sarah Stream, who was surprisingly nonchalant about doing something that most people wouldn't have done on a dare – spending time alone in a part of Malvern Manor that was said to be one of the most haunted.

She was gracious enough not to show any annoyance that we were interrupting her alone time with whatever it was that lurked up there.

"Think thin," Erik advised as the pair of us hauled

our not inconsiderably-sized frames up the rickety staircase.

"Never mind thin," I grumbled, "I'm trying to think *light.*"

Sarah had been conducting her own private EVP session, and had just said that Josh was going to be coming up to the attic later on. Immediately several voices were heard to say the word No.

"Yeah, whatever's up here doesn't seem to like me very much," he mused, stroking his chin thoughtfully. "I mean, *some* of the spirits at the Manor do like me..."

"Not up here," Sarah pointed out.

"What's that?" I said, holding up a hand to shush everybody. We could plainly hear the sound of scratching on one of the outer walls, which would have been part of the attic's roofing.

"Scratching," Stephen said. He was right. It was a slow, rhythmic scratching. We instantly perked up. Scratching sounds in the attic were one of the more commonly reported experiences that many visitors believed to be paranormal. The reality, however, turned out to be entirely more mundane; it was a breezy day, and the tips of the branches of the trees outside were scraping their way back and forth along the surface of the roof. No ghosts were needed to explain away this particular 'phenomenon.'

Although the attic was relatively bare, it was far from unfinished. Somebody had applied trim and baseboards, leading Josh to believe that the room had once served a very definite purpose above and beyond that of junk storage. What that purpose actually was, however, continued to elude him.

A now-defunct chimney dominated the center of the room. The top of it had been taken off, probably because it was the cause of the attic fire which had nearly burned the building down. Evidence of charring could still be seen on the roof beams when we looked upward.

Many visitors tended to find the attic to be a rather uncomfortable place to spend time. After no more than half an hour, many of them felt nauseous and had to leave. "Everybody but Sarah, apparently," Josh said, "who could practically live up here."

Sarah favored him with an enthusiastic smile. She could not possibly have known at the time that just one week later, she was due to have a frightening experience in the attic, one that would make her think twice about wanting to spend much time alone up there in the future. You will find that experience documented elsewhere in this book.

"Plenty of people have tossed their cookies up here," Josh said, indicating that more than a few visitors had vomited in the attic after being in that environment for an extended amount of time. "It's always super-fun for me to clean that up."

"You've puked up here too," Sarah pointed out, throwing him under the bus without a moment's hesitation.

"I came close," he admitted. "Luckily for me, when I figured out that I was about to lose my lunch, I was able to haul ass downstairs before it actually happened."

The repeated instances of vomiting made me wonder about the background EMF levels in the attic. Could we be dealing with a so-called fear cage – an area with extremely high electromagnetic energies, so much so that they would affect the human mind and body? Such places tended to generate feelings of being watched, the sensation of being touched by an invisible person, and if the EMF levels were high enough, could sometimes induce nausea and vomiting.

A quick sweep with our tri-field EMF meters soon demolished that theory. Although a certain amount of wiring did run through the attic, the levels of electromagnetic energy were pretty much unremarkable.

Other phenomena associated with the attic were

disembodied growls, and sometimes strange dragging noises, as though something heavy were being hauled from one end of the attic to the other. Neither of those auditory phenomena could be explained away by the scraping of branches along the outside of the roof.

"At first, I thought that the growling could have been some kind of animal – a raccoon, or something like that. I mean, the building is pretty old. There are certainly a few holes that critters could get in through. The growling usually seems to come from back here." Squatting down, he indicated a dark and confined crawlspace. "So I went back there to check, looking for animal droppings and stuff like that – not a thing."

Something I found fascinating was a collection of bottles that stood together in one of the corners. All of them had once contained alcohol of some description, ranging from cheap beer to Jack Daniels. Some enterprising visitor had surrounded them with an unbroken circle of salt.

"What I did find back there was a bunch of very personal items. Tobacco pouches; cigarettes; playing cards; lighters. Most of it seemed to date back to the 70s or the 80s. It makes me wonder if the residents might have been sneaking up here back in the day for a sly drink, smoke, or game of cards."

"What do you know about the entity that haunts the attic?" asked Erik.

"Whoever he is will try his best to get you back down those stairs. Because of the growling, and the fact that quite a few visitors have gotten scratched up here, a number of people have suggested that this particular haunting is demonic." Josh sighed, pausing to gather his thoughts. "I'm always very hesitant to throw out the D-word. What I think is going on here is a case of *peacocking*."

I'd never heard the term before. Used in this context, Josh explained that peacocking means that the male entity who is resident in the attic likes to scare people away from what he sees as his own personal turf as quickly as possible. To that end, he tends to puff himself up and growl in the ears of visitors as a way of instilling fear.

"As much as this guy wants you gone, he'll also beg you for alcohol and cigarettes. Hence the bottles of booze down there. We've gotten EVPs asking for those kind of addictive substances."

One day, Josh had left a digital voice recorder running at the top of the staircase leading up into the attic. He had gone to get himself some lunch, and come back later to pick up the device. Before leaving, he had called out, "Just give me ninety seconds to clear the building."

When he played back the audio file, he was astonished to discover that three minutes after he had walked away, the sound of heavy footsteps had started up. They were clearly heard to be walking across the wooden floor of the attic, getting closer and closer to the recorder. Then there came the noise of the recorder being jostled, as though somebody had picked the device up. After that, the file suddenly cut off. The implication was very clear: somebody had given Josh three minutes to get clear, and then moseyed across the attic and switched off the digital voice recorder. Josh had searched the attic thoroughly, and completely satisfied himself that whoever was responsible, it certainly hadn't been a flesh and blood human being who had snuck out of hiding to do it.

He was happy to have gotten some good paranormal evidence, but a little chagrined at the thought that he'd wasted 57 minutes of his lunch hour, not knowing that his recorder had been switched off.

Something a little more sinister happened during one of the day tours. Two female guests had wanted to spend a little time up in the attic. They sat with their backs to one of the walls, gazing into the near-darkness behind the roof beams, which made up a semi-concealed space between the floor and the pitched roof.

Suddenly, they were horrified to see a human arm emerge from the blackness. Nothing else was visible – just an arm. As if this wasn't bad enough, what freaked them out even more was that the arm then began to wave at them, beckoning them to come closer to it. Jumping to their feet and making ready to get the hell out of Dodge, the two young ladies heard shuffling coming from the hidden crawlspace off to their right. Looking over in that direction, they could hardly believe their eyes.

"As they told the story to us," Josh said, "they both saw what looked like a torso coming toward them out of the crawlspace. They said that it was dragging itself along, like something out of *The Walking Dead*. It had the face of a man, arms, but no legs. I'm pretty sure they're never going to come back here again."

Many people have had unnerving experiences up in the attic. Josh himself claims to have seen a man's face peering at him out of the shadows. This happened on the same day that he was overcome with nausea and had to bolt from the attic before vomiting.

That was a lot to think about, and a lot of ground for our team to cover over the space of just a few days and nights. We were glad that Josh had pointed out the hot spots to us, as it would help target our attention on those areas which were said to be the most paranormally active. We had only six people; it would be possible to put three or four times that many investigators inside Malvern Manor and still be unable to cover everything satisfactorily. It was simply that big.

But we'd give it our very best shot.

Chapter Eight
Rose the Haunted Doll

Back in Josh's office, we finished up our paperwork, grabbed blank copies of the waiver for Connie and Susan to sign when they got in, and Erik took custody of the keys to the Manor.

"Who's this?" I asked curiously, pointing at a creepy-looking child's doll that was sitting on a shelf. It was in a glass case with a lid on top, and had a distinctly *Annabelle*-esque air about it.

"Oh, that freakin' thing." Josh rolled his eyes. "That's Rose. Rose the haunted doll."

Four sets of ears immediately perked up at his use of the words 'haunted doll.'

Her story was an intriguing one. Rose had been donated to Josh by a friend who insisted that there was a spirit of some sort attached to it.

One day, Josh had gotten a phone call out of the blue from a lady who had visited Malvern Manor on a number of occasions. She had told him that he was the only person she felt comfortable calling about this particular issue, as he was the only paranormal investigator that she knew personally.

The lady went on to explain that she had obtained a doll which seemed to be at the center of some very strange activity. It would move from room to room in her house, without anybody actually having carried it there. She concluded by saying that she thought the doll was haunted, and asked Josh whether he would be willing to take custody of it.

Josh was only too happy to say yes. He took possession of the doll (see what I did there?) and wasted no time in placing it inside a Tupperware container, which he kept on a shelf inside one of the vacant rooms on the ground floor.

Coming in to do some work at the Manor a few days after taking custody of Rose, Josh was surprised to find that she was gone from her container. The top had been popped off and cast aside. Nobody had visited the place since he had last been there, so it was a complete mystery to him as to where the doll could possibly have gone.

Josh searched the Manor high and low. Finally, he discovered Rose sitting impishly in the middle of the hallway which led toward the nursing wing.

"Well, shit," was all he could find to say.

Deciding that a little more security was in order, Josh asked his grandfather to custom-make a glass display case for Rose, complete with a well-fitting lid. Rose now lives exclusively in the office at Malvern Manor, and although she tends to move around inside her glass case at night, she has yet to escape its confines. (It's worth pointing out that the office is always kept securely locked when unattended – there should be no feasible way for Rose to keep moving backwards and forward inside her case...yet somehow she still manages). Some days, Rose is found with her face smooshed against the glass; on others, she is slumped backwards with her legs doing the splits.

"Every time I put a camera on her overnight, she never moves an inch. Murphy's Law. Do you want to use her on the investigation?" Josh asked, taking the glass case down and carefully removing the lid. "She'd probably make one hell of a good control object."

Our eyes lit up at the prospect. Control objects are items of some sort of significance to the location in which they are used or to the spirits that are said to haunt it. Paranormal investigators place them at strategic locations throughout the building they are investigating and draw an outline around them, which helps to tell whether the control object has been moved. The hope is that the familiarity or appeal of the object will possibly entice the spirits to try and play with it or manipulate it. At the Denver Firefighters' Museum, I had used my old firefighters' helmet as a control object, for example. In cases where the spirit is believed to be that of a child, toys often serve the same purpose.

Carrying her through to the break room, we set Rose's case down on a table between two armchairs and took some reference photographs. Would Rose perform her party trick for us and move within the case all by herself? We really hoped so.

There was an angry, negative (some have used the word evil) spirit supposedly attached to Rose – an extremely unpleasant male voice which is given to growling and hurling insults. This entity has been nicknamed 'Number One' because, when asked its name during EVP sessions, that is the only reply to ever come through. Number One apparently likes to hijack Spirit Box sessions with its abusive and aggressive responses. Number One never put in an appearance until after Rose arrived at Malvern Manor, and it has been speculated that it might be the source of the dark energy up on the second floor.

"We haven't heard from Number One in three or

four weeks," Josh told us, "and hopefully he won't give you any trouble while you're here. Be aware that he's kind of a dick..."

"Do you have any suggestions for how best to approach this investigation?" I asked.

"It will make you chase it," Sarah said, rather ominously, I thought. Josh nodded his agreement.

"You'll play a lot of cat and mouse," Josh repeated. "Expect this place to run you ragged."

"What are the top three areas, in terms of paranormal activity?"

Josh counted them off on his fingers. "The Attic. The nursing home wing, for sure. And the Captain's Corner. Those are the big three that I'd hit." Wishing us the best of luck, Josh gave us his cell phone number and told us to call him if we needed anything. With that, he and Sarah turned and left us to our own devices. Erik locked the door behind them.

We were all alone, locked down inside Malvern Manor for the night.

Chapter Nine
Bleeding

While Jill was getting some of her gear together, Stephen, Erik and I were standing around in the kitchen, checking our equipment in advance of the forthcoming evening's investigation.

It was essential to make sure that every disposable battery was either factory fresh and straight out of the packaging or, in the case of the permanent batteries, was fully-charged to maximum capacity. Unexplained power drains are the bane of the paranormal investigator, but there's an up-side to that too – at least one theory states that the missing electricity is somehow converted into another form of energy that may be used to power paranormal activity, in what may be a case of the spirits using a free source of power for their own purposes. Speaking for myself, I'd be very okay with the ghosts of Malvern Manor using as much of my battery supply as they wanted if it meant I'd get to witness something paranormal.

The kitchen door slammed back on its hinges, admitting a slightly agitated Jill. She had one hand clasped to the left side of her head. Traces of bright red blood were visible on her fingers; not a great deal of the stuff – it's not as though she was in any real danger – but its presence was a little worrying.

"Jill, what happened?" Stephen asked, plainly concerned.

"I don't know! My ear just started bleeding, and I don't know why."

"Let me take a look," I said, gently moving Jill's hand away from her ear. I'm a paramedic by profession and I've seen a lot of lacerations, both major and minor. This was one of the smaller variety, making it more a source of puzzlement than any sort of real threat. It was a small horizontal cut to the fleshy part of her outer ear, bubbling with blood. Normally I would expect it to have already begun to clot by now, but as the cut was continuing to bleed, I recommended that Jill hold direct pressure on it for a few more minutes.

"Did you cut that on anything when you were outside?" Stephen wanted to know. "Like a tree branch or something? Or maybe you caught it on something when Josh was giving us the grand tour."

"No," Jill insisted, shaking her head. "If I'd grazed

my ear on something, I'm sure that I would have felt it, especially if it was hard enough to draw blood."

I had to admit that Jill had a point. The ear is a very sensitive part of the body. Even something as small as a paper-cut there should have been painful enough to make her aware that it had happened.

"Were you scratching your ear, maybe?" I suggested. Again, Jill shook her head.

"No, I wasn't. And my hair usually covers my ears anyway." Jill had shoulder-length hair which did indeed fall in front of her ears most of the time. This was a bit of a puzzler. None of us could figure out quite how this had happened, and we couldn't help but wonder whether this was one of the resident spirits of Malvern Manor signaling their disapproval at our presence in the building. If so, it was going to be majorly disappointed, because we would be there for the next three nights, and if it thought that we were being annoying now...

Jill decided that it might be best if she put her rosary on, giving her an extra layer of spiritual protection. She slipped it on over her neck and seemed to feel a little better.

"If that was you, go ahead and harm another one of our investigators," Stephen said, talking to thin air. "Go ahead and do something to me."

The words hung there, an explicit challenge for any of the less-benevolent spirits that might be willing to square off against us. Now all that remained was to see whether any of them were going to take the bait.

After ten minutes or so, the small wound had clotted sufficiently for Jill to be able to take her hand away. We decided to give Room 7 a try. Josh had talked about the door opening on command, shadow figures being seen peeking around the edge of the door-frame, and that the door was supposedly haunted by a screaming woman who had pulled all of her own hair out because she believed that her husband and family had abandoned her.

Heading over to the nursing home wing, we made ourselves as comfortable as possible in the empty room and began an EVP session, using digital voice recorders and an Ovilus IV as our basic tools.

We began to ask a series of questions, the usual generic sort of thing used by paranormal investigators all around the world. Is there anybody here that wishes to communicate with us? What's your name? Can you say the name of any of those who are present?

In apparent response, the Ovilus said, *Leave. Now.*

We looked at one another with raised eyebrows. The forlorn lady who was said to haunt this room was reportedly very unhappy when male visitors encroached upon her space. There were now three men and one woman in her room. Could she perhaps be telling us to get out?

Unfortunately, none of the roughly thirty-second burst sessions we conducted yielded any EVPs in Room 7.

"Maybe she's feeling a little crowded," Stephen mused. "Why don't the three of you head on out of here for a while and check out the rest of the Manor? I'll stay here and see whether I get better results on my own."

That sounded like a plan to us. Jill, Erik and I went back to the main building and made our way up to the second floor.

"This thing kind of creeps me out," Jill said as we climbed the staircase at the best speed that could be expected of three middle-aged, out-of-shape paranormal investigators.

"Why? Because it's rickety?" I asked.

"Because the bannister's so low?" Erik added, patting the handrail.

"Kind of," she agreed. "If something were to push

you..."

"Well, thanks for putting that idea right out there in the open," I grumbled, my imagination now working overtime and picturing some type of angry entity shoving one of us over the balcony with invisible hands. "Thanks a bunch."

"Just hug the wall," Jill smirked, not sounding the least bit sorry.

Reaching the second floor without anybody taking a swan dive, we proceeded to roam the empty rooms and hallways, just getting a feel for the place. The daylight was fading quickly outside, and without any lights being switched on, everything looked gloomy and drab. It may have been nothing more than a product of our imagination, but we began to feel that the atmosphere was beginning to change, becoming a little more...charged, for lack of a better word. There was a definite feeling of not being alone in there.

Without any particular objective in mind, we wandered across to Hank's room. Jill pulled open the drawer and picked up one of his shirts. I winced.

"Wow, Hank – I wouldn't let a woman touch any of my clothes. She'll probably make a right mess of it."

"Oh, please," Jill said, playing along. "I'm the world's best shirt folder. Bet I can do a better job than you."

From there, we went on further down the hallway, poking our heads into rooms 16 and 17 before then moving on toward the attic doorway. We found still more children's shoes scattered about the place, most of them in some very odd locations.

We agreed to save the attic for later, and after looking inside every single room on the second floor, made our way back downstairs to the parlor, which seemed to lack the odd ambience that we were picking up on upstairs.

"There's the chair that Katrina slept in," Erik pointed out.

"You know what – she was right," I said, sinking into the soft leather seat with a sigh that is familiar to middle-aged people everywhere, "It really is comfortable."

Jill settled into one of the two wheelchairs that was said to move of its own volition. We sat there comfortably for a moment. It was then that Erik made the ill-advised decision to shine a black-light on the various chairs. The sheer amount of unidentified fluid staining each of them made Jill and I practically leap to our feet. Some questions really are better left unanswered...

Chapter Ten
A Moan in the Dark

As things turned out, Stephen got precious little in the way of results during the time he spent alone in the nursing home wing. When we rejoined him, he had just finished up a solo EVP session in Gracie's room. He told us excitedly that he had gotten some very faint but audible whispering in response to his questions.

"I really do feel that we're going to get some activity going on here tonight," Stephen said. At that very moment, I got the intense chills, that feeling which some people like to describe as, 'Oh, somebody just walked over my grave.' Although this could have been completely psychological, my body seemed to be in agreement with what Stephen was saying.

The sound of footsteps growing closer heralded the arrival of the remainder of our team.

Connie was a perky, perpetually-cheerful lady who made a living in the legal field, whereas Susan was an aerospace engineer that could quite literally claim to be a rocket scientist. Both were experienced paranormal investigators who had great senses of humor and were pretty much unflappable – exactly the sort of company you wanted to keep at a place like Malvern Manor.

We wasted no time in filling Connie and Susan in on everything that Josh had told us, finishing up with Jill's mysterious ear bleed. They found what little kitchen surface space remained and laid out their own equipment. We certainly didn't lack for gadgetry, although I've always believed that great evidence can often be gathered using little more than an audio recorder, an inquiring mind, and an astute line of questioning.

As they were both famished, we locked up the Manor and headed across the road to a very pleasant cafe. It was already dark outside, and so we left the kitchen light on. All of the others were switched off. After eating a hearty dinner (more than enough to last us through until breakfast the following morning) we made our way back over to the Manor again.

As hard as it was to believe, light was streaming out of a window on the second floor.

"We definitely switched off all those lights before we came out, right?" Stephen said. Everybody confirmed that we all had, in fact, left nothing but the kitchen light on.

So how on Earth had the upstairs landing light gotten switched on?

"Maybe a timer?" Erik suggesting, sounding unconvinced.

"Not likely," I replied, shaking my head, "We were here last night at around the same time and the light never came on."

We subsequently confirmed that none of the lights in the house were on an automatic timer. All of them were operated manually.

After a brief discussion about where to start out, the six of us settled upon conducting an EVP session over on the nursing home side. Grabbing a plastic five-gallon bucket apiece (they make for great portable seating, as well as being a very handy way to carry a lot of ghost-hunting equipment) we trooped over to the nurse's station. It was pitch black down there, thanks to the lack of ambient light, and the air was freezing cold – nothing paranormal, but simply a result of how badly-insulated that particular wing of the building was. It was a late addition to the structure, and not part of the original construction.

The majority of the actual nurse's station had been torn out by a former owner, but fragments of it still remained. A series of wooden pigeonholes that must once have been used to store patient charts and medications still bore the names of the last occupants. I stood quietly for a moment, reading each name by flashlight. The poignancy and significance of those pigeonholes was not lost on me; each one represented a human life, a living, breathing person who had lived at Malvern Manor for who knew how long? Every one of them had their own unique story to tell. Most were almost certainly dead by now, but some could still be alive, perhaps living in nearby facilities. I hoped that their time here was as happy and peaceful as possible.

There was a lot of activity reported on this side of the building. Of great interest to us was Room 2, outside which the Shadow Man was said to appear. The room was currently locked up and being used for private storage, but as Josh had told us, during the time the nursing wing was operational, it was home to a man that almost the entire staff was deathly afraid of. This particular patient was a big, powerful man with a history of very aggressive psychotic behavior – in fact, he was said to have killed two people prior to his arrival at Malvern Manor. The staff were so intimidated by this silent giant that he was the only patient who was never made to put on his shoes when he was up and walking about.

Josh had warned us that the Shadow Man had been encountered by more than one visitor, and always seemed to behave in the same aggressive way. Was this big black shape the ghost of the man who had scared so many nurses during his lifetime, doing the same thing to intrusive ghost hunters years after his death? It certainly made sense to me. After all, the apparition always seemed to materialize at the same point in the hallway, right outside the door of Room 2. However, there was another interesting possibility on the table here, and what brought it to mind was the way in which the shadowy form seemed to behave – with complete consistency. In other words, according to the eyewitness accounts, it seemed to act in precisely the same way each time it was encountered, always appearing at the same location, following the same path, and disappearing right in front of the person who saw it.

Rather than being an intelligent spirit, could this instead be a residual haunting – in other words, a type of paranormal 'recording' that was somehow triggered and played back when certain circumstances arose? To the best of my knowledge, there were no reports of the so-called Shadow Man directly interacting with anybody, or trying to communicate with them in any way.

It had reportedly taken Johnny Houser a solid two hours of standing in the same place, staring into the darkness at the end of the hall, and waiting patiently, for the Shadow Man to finally manifest. Placing our five-gallon buckets face-down on the ground, we each took our seats and started a bunch of digital voice recorders running, positioned at various points along the hallway.

As best we could, we wanted to watch both ends of the hallway at the same time, because a room at the opposite end – number 7 – had an equally fascinating history. The story attached to this room is a deeply sad and tragic one, as it was said to be the home of a beautiful woman who was at the nursing home for an extended stay. This poor lady somehow developed the notion that her beauty had faded and that as a result, her husband no longer loved her. The thought of it made her so distressed that she began to brush her hair over and over again. When this didn't make her feel any better, she started to tear it out by the fistful.

If this story is true – and like so many other stories associated with the Manor, its source is anecdotal – then one can only imagine the loneliness, fear, and pain that she must have felt. When Josh had recounted the tale to us, it was a truly saddening thing to hear. In more recent times, visiting paranormal investigators have seen shadowy figures at the end of the hallway, sometimes surreptitiously peeking out of Room 7 at the newcomers, before darting back inside again. Whenever anybody goes to check, the room is always empty.

Although most of our attention was focused on the Shadow Man's part of the hallway, I kept turning my head to look in the opposite direction toward Room 7. Whether this was a purely psychological reaction to having my back turned on a dark and supposedly haunted hallway, or a genuine sense of something invisible being present, I cannot say for sure; but there was a definite air of unease about that end of the nursing wing. As the old cliche goes, you felt as if you were being watched.

The atmosphere was a little on the oppressive side, so we deliberately kept things as fun and light as possible, cracking bad jokes and laughing at them. Some paranormal investigators tend to adopt an extremely serious, almost dour approach, and if that works for them, then it's all well and good; speaking personally, I started out that way twenty-six years ago, but I've gradually lightened up since then, having come to the conclusion that laughter and humor seem to provide their own form of positive energy. Sometimes you get the very best results when you're all sitting around and just BSing. Besides, I spend (some people would say *waste*) a great deal of my time carrying out paranormal field research, and as with so many other things in life, if you can't have some fun doing it then what's the point?

The six of us carried on staring off into the darkness, giving our eyes the chance to adjust. Every once in a while, we would hear the sound of a passing car and see some of the light given off by its high-beams filtering through the grimy windows.

"Is there anybody down there?" asked Jill, peering down the length of the deserted hallway.

"Not after this freak-show just rolled into town," Erik grumbled, *sotto voce*. The rest of us chuckled.

Then the gastric sounds started. Nobody was quite sure whose stomach rumbled first, but that opened the floodgates, and before long we were all at it, a chorus of low growls, each of one having to be marked on the digital voice recordings so that we did not mistake them for something else during the evidence review phase of our investigation.

Finally, our bellies shut up. Quiet returned to the

nursing wing once more. We all took turns in politely asking for some sort of sign that anybody might be present, making a point of using a very respectful tone of voice.

We were also running an Ovilus device in the background. In case you're unfamiliar with it, the Ovilus is – according to those who are proponent of it – capable of detecting fluctuations in the energy levels all around it and assigning each specific energy reading to a word in its internal dictionary. The upshot of this is said to be that some spirits may be capable of manipulating those energy fields so precisely that they can actually spell out meaningful words and phrases.

To say that the Ovilus is a controversial device would be putting it mildly. It certainly has its share of supporters, but it doesn't lack for detractors either. Those who claim that the Ovilus is simply a 'random word generator,' for want of a better term, like to point out that there is no substantial theory to explain exactly how a discarnate entity could somehow read the entries in the device's onboard dictionary, and then attune the energies around the Ovilus in order to spit out words that make any kind of sense.

I used to be in the same camp as those who thought

that the Ovilus was nothing more than a gimmick. After all, the device puts out nonsensical and irrelevant words at least 95% of the time. I had seen some stellar hits, but then even a broken clock will tell the correct time twice a day, so wouldn't the Ovilus statistically have those impressive results every once in a while? As with psychic readings, human nature tends to focus on the hits rather than the misses. Does a handful of very close to the mark results really outweigh a mountain of absolute gibberish?

But then, a rather curious thing happened. I found that the more I used the Ovilus, the more frequently those impressive hits became. Working on a private case in an ordinary town-home where had been a particularly ugly murder-suicide in which a mother and her child were said to have been drowned in the bathtub, the Ovilus began to pipe up with such words as *Drowned, Wet,* and *Water.* When I went upstairs to investigate the bathroom in which the drownings had taken place, the words *Three Upstairs* came out of the box. Coincidence...or something else? During the same case, one of my fellow investigators was stunned when her clothing developed a significantly-sized wet patch on it. (For full particulars of the case, the reader is referred to my book *Trail of Terror,* or the episode of *Haunted Case Files* which dramatized those events).

Not long afterward, I was fortunate enough to spend a week investigating a haunted inn just outside Gettysburg. The inn was built close to the site of a major cavalry action, and had been pressed into service as a Confederate field hospital to take care of the wounded and dying from that brutal engagement. A plaque mounted on the wall said that a battery of Confederate artillery had been stationed at the inn on July 4, 1863. The Ovilus came out with the words *Southern Cannon*. Yet again, quite the coincidence (assuming that you believe in such things) or something else? That is left for the reader to decide for themselves.

The atmosphere in the nursing wing was still pretty flat, with nothing remotely paranormal taking place, so far as we could see. Being the natural raconteur that he is, Stephen began telling us a pretty off-color story about a recent investigation that he'd been on. It painted a couple of the people involved in a fairly unflattering light.

Jerk, commented the Ovilus. Suitably chastened, Stephen quickly changed the subject. It would not be the last time that this strange little gadget would raise eyebrows at Malvern Manor.

The moan took us all by surprise. Low and

mournful, it came from somewhere in the darkness behind us.

"What the hell was *that?*" Six heads whipped round toward the open doorway of Room 7. I played the beam of my flashlight around that end of the hallway. Room 7 and its neighbors were, just as you would expect in a haunted old building, completely empty.

"That was a moan," Erik said, stating the obvious.

We had multiple digital voice recorders running simultaneously. There was a mad scramble to play back the audio file. We hooked up our first voice recorder to an external speaker. Sure enough, there it was: a definite moan. Whether male or female, it was impossible to say with any confidence. It sounded a lot like the noise that an older person might make if they were in distress and needed help. It had definitely not come from any of the investigators present, and had been picked up on multiple recorders.

Perhaps it was a completely residual audio phenomenon, or perhaps we weren't alone in the nursing wing after all.

Just as Stephen had predicted earlier, Malvern Manor appeared to be waking up.

Chapter Eleven
Coloring with Suzie

Our sense of anticipation continued to grow.

Yet there were no more inexplicable moans or other noises, and after another half-hour had passed, we took some time out to do an equipment check. Bizarrely, I discovered that my digital voice recorder had somehow lost about six hours' worth of battery charge in just thirty minutes of recording time. To compound things even further, exactly the same thing had happened to Stephen's TASCAM DR5 recorder, which went down 90% in the same amount of time. To put that number in perspective, it usually takes somewhere around ten hours for that level of battery drain to take place.

Nor were Stephen and I the only ones whose recording gear was so affected. We would discover later on that out in the parlor, the digital voice recorder that Erik had left on the wheelchair (the one which likes to move itself) had drained from having a completely full, factory-fresh battery to being completely dead in only three hours. The recorder was a very efficient device when it came down to power usage, and with fresh batteries usually lasted for a full twenty-four hours at a bare minimum, and often for much longer.

It appeared that either something was leeching our equipment of its electrical energy. We were optimistic that wherever that energy had gone, it might very well serve as a great source of power for the ghosts of Malvern Manor to manifest with.

Sticking with the nursing wing for a while longer, we made specific attempts to address the Shadow Man directly. Our hope was to draw him out, but for whatever reason, he didn't seem to be in the mood to materialize and charge at any of us. There were no more moans or cries. We decided to spend a few minutes in the break room, getting warm after the chilliness of the nursing wing, and debated where we should investigate next over some hot beverages.

We finally settled on Suzie's room for our next point of focus. I had found the story of this poor lady to be very touching. She was said to be an adult middle-aged woman in body, but with the mind of an eight year old child. She liked nothing better than to color in pictures, and the mattress that lay on the floor of her room was festooned with coloring books of all varieties, along with an assortment of pens and crayons. Some paranormal investigators had reported getting good EVP results when they sat down to color with Suzie, talking kindly and gently to her. On their last visit, the AAPI team had asked Suzie what her favorite color was, and had gotten an EVP saying the word, *Pink.* They had therefore brought her a pink Easter basket and some goodies to play with. Jill set the offering carefully down on the bed and then sat down on the floor in front of it.

The room was small, which made it a tight squeeze for six of us, so we alternated taking turns standing outside in the hallway. Like most of the rooms at Malvern Manor, Suzie's room was cold, grimy, and hadn't been cleaned in quite some time.

We set a couple of EVP recorders running and placed a REM-POD on the mattress. The REM-POD is basically an EMF meter that detects electromagnetic fields and then puts out both audio and visual alarms. The stronger the EMF levels (and the closer they are to the device), the longer and more intense the alarm.

Jill took the lead in asking Suzie questions, starting with her favorite color (was it still pink?) and progressing to her likes and dislikes. We worked in 30-second bursts, playing them back immediately afterward. Although we had all heard a creaking sound outside in the corridor, I thought that it was simply the structure shifting, something that very commonly happens at night when the construction materials cool down and contract.

On playback, there was nothing of note; no discernible EVPs of any kind. I took my turn doing the next short burst session. According to Josh, investigators had gotten EVPs in the past saying that Suzie couldn't leave her room because he (whoever 'he' was) wouldn't allow her to. I asked who was keeping Suzie confined to her room. Was it perhaps the Captain, who had a reputation for being very dominant up on there the second floor?

It was only after the burst was over that I had a sort of epiphany: I had been working on the assumption that whoever was responsible for keeping Suzie cooped up in her room was doing so for ominous reasons. What if this was actually a good-natured spirit, one who wanted her to stay in there for her own protection? Based on the stories we had been told about something dark and malevolent also haunting the second floor, could her captor actually be trying to keep her safe? Clearly, more investigation was needed.

I continued with this line of questioning.

"Who is it that wouldn't let you out of this room?"

No sooner was the question out of my mouth than

the REM-POD began to go off, its audio alarm (a loud and thoroughly annoying electronic chirp) accompanied by an array of flashing colored lights that strobed across the walls and mattress.

"Is everybody's phone in airplane mode?" I asked, finding the timing a little suspicious. It turned out that not everybody's phone was shut down, which meant that if the phone was sending a call, sending a text, or trying to communicate with a nearby cell tower, it would be putting out a strong enough signal to set the REM-POD off.

Cursing, the team made doubly sure that all of our phones were now locked down, which meant that there would be no electromagnetic transmissions coming from any of them.

Still the REM-POD continued to go berserk. Now, that was puzzling. Some other source of electromagnetic energy had to be responsible, but what? Having ruled out all of our portable electronic devices, we were left with whatever might be running inside the Manor itself. Although there was a wi-fi network installed there, it hadn't triggered the REM-POD before now. All of the computer equipment was on the ground floor, not the second, and the wireless signal strength was pretty poor up there. Try as we might, we could identify no source for the EMF spike.

Malvern's firehouse was just a few hundred feet down the street. If the fire truck happened to be going out and transmitting on its vehicle-mounted radio set, then it was entirely possible that those radio emissions could be responsible. But there were no lights, no sirens, and no signs of life coming from the firehouse, which was a volunteer station rather than being continuously manned around the clock. It was highly unlikely that somebody would be in there transmitting on a radio set this late at night (it was close to midnight) and unless there happened to be a ham radio operator who was working a powerful set, I didn't see a good reason for the way that the device was behaving.

When the batteries on a REM-POD start to get very low, the device will often emit an alarm. These batteries were fresh.

"Suzie, if that's you, could you please step away from the flashing lights?" Jill asked. The REM-POD wasn't inclined to acquiesce. Sighing, Jill tried again. "Alright, if that's somebody else, please step away."

The REM-POD kept alarming for another twenty seconds or so, then finally died. We all looked at one another, nonplussed.

"Suzie, can you please step forward and make the box light up again?" Jill requested. The REM-POD obstinately refused to comply. Josh's words came back to mind: *This place likes to play cat and mouse with you. It'll dangle stuff in front of you, just enough to get you interested, and then draw back. Happens all the time.*

A sudden, sharp intake of breath startled Stephen – mainly because it had come from outside in the corridor, from what sounded like the direction of Inez's room. He stuck his head outside and found nobody there. We had all heard it, captured it on three different voice recorders, and were certain that it hadn't come from one of us.

"Whoever's out in the hallway, come on in here," Stephen said, raising his voice. "I know you're there. I keep hearing you moving around out there, and I can sense you. Don't be afraid. Come on in here and talk to us, please."

Convinced that there was some kind of entity lurking just outside in the darkened corridor, Stephen tried to coax it into coming into Suzie's room and communicating with us. Had it been the source of the inhalation that we had all just heard?

After fifteen minutes of frustrating attempts at coaxing brought no results, we decided that another break was in order. Stephen sensed that the entity was still out there, holding its ground and keeping an eye on us. It apparently wasn't willing to be drawn out. While Stephen, Connie, Susan and I made our way back down to the break room, Jill and Erik hung back for just a minute or two longer, hoping that the reduction in numbers might make our unseen watcher a little less shy.

Just as Stephen was firing up the electric kettle to get some hot tea going, the sound of pounding footsteps on the main staircase made us all look up. While they hadn't exactly run away, Jill and Erik had been effectively chased all the way down the staircase by the invisible entity.

"That thing was right on our tail!" Jill insisted, pushing the hanging curtain aside and walking into the break room. She was somewhat agitated, breathing a little rapidly after what had just happened. To borrow a phrase, she looked as if she had seen a ghost, thanks to the massive adrenaline dump jolt that she had just undergone.

"How do you know it was on your tail?" I asked, ever the skeptic.

"It was such an intense feeling, I got that fight or flight response. My instincts told me to flee."

Fascinated, I asked whether it was at the foot of the

staircase right now.

"It stopped at about halfway down the stairs," Erik explained. He had sensed it too, though not as acutely as Jill had. When it comes to being sensitive, Erik is a little more cautious; he likes to keep his protective barriers up when investigating a location, particularly one where the presence of darker energies is suspected.

"It waited for us outside Suzie's room, hanging around until the four of you had gone, and then chased us all the way down the hall, coming up right behind us and pushing us along every step of the way. We started speeding up to get away from it, and it picked up its pace to match ours."

I watched Jill carefully, trying to read her body language. She was clearly a little agitated, but maintaining a completely professional affect nonetheless – something that was only to be expected of a good paranormal investigator. As a paramedic, I get lied to for a living (it's amazing how many severely intoxicated patients have "just had two beers, I swear") and I like to think that I've developed a pretty good radar for bullshit. Jill was coming across as completely genuine from where I was sitting.

A loud metallic twang from the kitchen made us all

jump. I realized right away what it was: my can of Monster energy drink had just popped. It happened all the time with those cans, and there was nothing remotely paranormal about it. Still, it never failed to make me jump.

Erik's version of the story was practically identical. "Jill kept saying that it was behind us, and I refused to run from it. I was in front and she was behind me. I stopped in place to let Jill catch up, and when she did, I felt it – a wave of energy run through my entire body, making it buzz as though I'd been hit with an electric current. I could actually feel the back of my tongue tingling, almost as if I'd just licked a 9-volt battery.

"You used to work in I.T, right?" Erik asked me. I nodded. "Have you ever been in one of those huge data-centers that are basically a collection of big server farms? The air in those places is highly charged. You can just feel it. That's exactly what this felt like. It filled the entire hall."

After dissecting and analyzing Jill and Erik's experience, we finally localized the beginning of the phenomenon to the part of the second floor hallway – the same section in which the spirit of the Captain was most commonly encountered. Could this perhaps be him, expressing his displeasure at our presence or the things that we were doing? After all, Josh had told us during our initial walkthrough that the Captain disliked ghost hunters in general.

"I was bringing up the rear of the first group," Susan chimed in, "and I definitely felt a little weird. I mean, nothing as intense as what these guys felt, but it was something very strange. It certainly made me uncomfortable."

"This thing was *massive,*" Jill said, and Erik added that it was also very cold, causing a noticeable temperature drop. The two investigators had paused before reaching the landing and turned around, shining their flashlights behind them. They couldn't see anything, and got the distinct impression that the energy form was waiting for them to make their next move.

Enough talking – it was time to see whether the thing was still there. Considering it unwise to go alone, I asked Connie to accompany me back upstairs to see if we would experience anything similar. I wasn't too optimistic about our chances (I'm about as psychically sensitive as the average house brick) but I figured it was worth a try. I wanted to keep the number of investigators to just two, as that was the number that had drawn the thing out the first time around. To bring more people might overwhelm it.

We didn't feel much of anything as we made our way carefully up the stairs. The lights stayed off. My heart was pounding in my ears as we climbed, with myself in the lead and Connie watching my back. Nothing was showing up in the beam of my flashlight. Reaching the top, we began to prowl the second floor corridors and rooms, starting with the stretch that led to Suzie's room and that of Inez.

"Who just chased our friends down the stairs?" I demanded, raising my voice. "Who – or what – are you?"

Other than a light breeze outside the windows, there was no response.

"I'm going to assume that most of the spirits here at Malvern Manor are friendly and good people," I went on, trying a different tack, "and I'm also going to assume that whoever or whatever just followed my friends didn't intend to frighten or harm them." I didn't necessarily believe that, but what the hell – sometimes you caught more flies with honey than with vinegar, as the old saying went.

"Maybe it just wanted time alone," Connie suggested. She may have been right about that. Neither of us were picking up on anything strange, certainly nothing like an invisible presence.

"We're friendly and we are trying to talk to you respectfully," I said. "Would you please talk to us?"

Apparently not.

Finally admitting defeat, we went back to the break room.

"It didn't take the bait with just two of us," Stephen pointed out. "Why don't we *all* go back up there and see how it reacts?"

Everybody agreed that it sounded like a good idea, and so the six of us made ourselves as comfortable as possible in the vicinity of the Captain's corner, giving ourselves good visibility along both directions of the corridor.

While she was more than willing to use her natural sensitivity as part of the investigation, Jill also elected to break out the SLS camera. This device (SLS stands for *Structured Light Sensor*) is one of the most controversial pieces of equipment that can be fielded by a paranormal investigator. With a price tag running anywhere from $400 to $1200, it also happens to be one of the most expensive.

The device throws out hundreds of pinpricks of infra-red (IR) light in front of it. When seen through the viewfinder of an infra-red camera, this looks like a spectacular barrage of polka dots being splashed across whatever reflective surface the SLS happens to be aimed at. If you happen to own an XBox that has a Kinect attached to it, you've seen this very same technology at work in the comfort of your own home.

Stand in front of the SLS camera and you start reflecting those IR beams right back into its sensor. The software loaded into the device perceives that there is a human-shaped form standing (or squatting, or sitting) in front of it, and then tries to make sense of the pattern by creating a stick-figure equivalent of that person. The SLS's sense of depth perception works a bit like radar or sonar; by measuring as precisely as possible the amount of time it takes for each IR return to bounce back from the human body into the sensor, the device can calculate with a surprising degree of accuracy exactly how far that particular body part is from the camera – and therefore, its relative position in the room.

Paranormal investigators use the SLS in the hope that those same infrared beams will somehow be able to bounce back from a spirit entity, and therefore be detectable by the camera's sensor. As some ghost photographs have been taken using IR cameras in the past, this raises an intriguing possibility – perhaps the SLS can perceive and record entities or energies that the human eye cannot.

But there's a problem, and that problem is pareidolia, which is the bane of any paranormal investigator that happens to be even the slightest bit skeptical. Pareidolia is a perfectly natural sensory process which depends upon the fact that the brain is essentially pre-wired to want to see the human face or body in what are actually random patterns. Perhaps the best example of this is the Man in the Moon, the fun misperception that a face is looking down at us from the surface of our planet's biggest satellite. We've all seen it, and once you have seen it, it is virtually impossible to un-see it. Your brain keeps going back to that face when you look up into the night sky.

Pareidolia is also the reason why so many people believe that they see faces in the clouds, flames, or columns of smoke, in addition to being responsible for practically all of those 'I see a face in this orb' claims, which almost always turn out to be camera flash reflections from specks of dust. The eye wants to see what the eye wants to see, and sometimes common sense doesn't seem to get a vote.

The SLS suffers from its own case of pareidolia, thanks to its programming. The device is conditioned to look for anything that somewhat approximates the human form, and then tends to misperceive it as being a living person. I have personally seen the SLS mistake a vertical pipe, the hard vertical edge of a doorframe, and a standing floor lamp for a human being. The SLS can be fooled, and quite easily fooled, if it isn't used correctly – or if its results are misinterpreted.

With that having been said, I have also seen the same type of camera detect what looks to be an extremely human-looking form in locations where there were no obvious features that could be easily misinterpreted. Clearly more research is needed into the way that the SLS-type camera system works, and so far as I am concerned, the jury is still out with regard to its use as a tool for investigating haunted locations. Speaking personally, whenever there is doubt concerning a particular tool or technique but that tool or technique may still yield results that are potentially paranormal, I will generally ignore the controversy and make use of it anyway. You never know when it might produce that kick-ass piece of evidence that is the Holy Grail for all paranormal investigators.

Firing up her own portable SLS, Jill used it to sweep the second floor hallways in both directions. It recognized her fellow investigators easily enough, mapping us into the system.

"Oh, *heeeeeello,*" she said when the SLS detected a stick figure in the middle of the hallway. Peering over her shoulder, I could see the figure itself, and could see that it was standing in a completely empty section of the corridor. The figure was big – at least seven feet tall – and had a head, arms, legs, and a torso. After a few seconds it disappeared, then phased right back in again. Other than a doorway, which the figure wasn't affixed to, there weren't any vertical structural features that might explain it away.

We each took turns in asking questions, trying to ascertain the figure's identity – if it was indeed an entity, and not simply the SLS seeing things. Was this the Captain, or Number One, we asked? (At this point, Erik couldn't resist making a *Star Trek* joke).

The stick figure came closer and closer to Jill, increasing in size until it loomed right up in front of her. She exhaled slowly but stood her ground. Bringing up my camera, I fired off three flash photographs in quick succession. It was disappointing to see that nothing anomalous appeared in any of them. A large part of me was hoping that the camera would have captured a huge shadow figure, or even better, a full-bodied apparition. Instead, all that it caught was a creepy-looking hallway.

We stayed like that for at least five minutes.

"Would you shake my hand?" I asked, more in an attempt to break the deadlock than anything. I extended a hand. The figure did not move. Jill and I both took a step forward. "Alright, we're coming forward to say hello to you."

Instantly the figure bolted, dashing toward the nearest open doorway, which led into Suzie's room. We were right on its heels, but the room was completely bare as far as the SLS was concerned. Whatever the figure had been, it was gone now.

Remember, this thing likes to play cat and mouse games...

Josh had been absolutely right. Frustrated, we went back out into the hallway. Jill aimed the SLS camera in the direction of Inez's room.

"There it is again," she said, shaking her head. "It just ducked its head out of Inez's room, then disappeared back inside."

Jill and Susan went after it, while the rest of us tagged along behind them both.

"We're not trying to corner you," Susan called out in an attempt to placate it. "We're just trying to communicate with you."

"This camera helps us to see you," Jill added.

As if on cue, an extremely tall stick figure emerged from inside Inez's room. It stood motionless for a moment, and then when Jill and Susan stepped toward it again, went right back inside.

"I'm getting that buzzing sensation again," Jill said, walking into Inez's room. "There's something in here. I know there is."

Sure enough, the figure was standing directly in front of the closet door. Filing in behind her, we all noticed that the temperature in there was much colder than anywhere else on the second floor.

Equally interesting was the stick figure's behavior. It was frantically waving its arms above its head, as though grappling with something at the topmost part of the closet. This was exactly what the stick figure had done the last time AAPI had used the SLS in this room, one year before.

"What's weird about this is that I was just telling Connie about what happened last year in Inez's room," Erik said, sounding impressed, "and now it looks like this stick figure is trying to recreate it for us."

"Are you Otto?" Jill asked, referring to the Inez's younger brother. "Are you trying to help Inez?"

The stick figure appeared to be pointing repeatedly up at the top shelf of the closet. We were trying to figure out whether this was a genuine anomaly or a false positive. Then a second figure appeared, standing alongside the first. There was an initial moment of excitement, until I realized that the newcomer tracked with the closet's doorframe exactly. That still didn't explain away the first figure, though, which could be seen in the middle of the doorway.

And just like that, the figures were gone, leaving us trying to determine what it was we'd just seen – a false positive from the SLS system software; a repeat of AAPI's experience the year before (minus the Geobox proclaiming "She's down!"); or something else?

Chapter Twelve
Nobody's Home

After another break, during which we took the opportunity to install some fresh sets of batteries, we opted to split up into two teams. Stephen, Jill, and Suzie went upstairs to conduct an EVP session up on the second floor, while Erik, Connie, and I elected to spend some time in Gracie's room.

Many visitors have spoken of there being unusual smells and an oppressive atmosphere in that particular room, but for my part, the atmosphere felt fine and I could smell nothing beyond the old musty odor that permeated most of the rooms at Malvern Manor.

Gingerly, I sat down on Gracie's bed, trying not to think of how many people had sat or lain on the same old mattress. Connie sat at the opposite end. She was more than a little thrilled by the fact that the last person to sleep on that bed was *Paranormal Lockdown*'s Nick Groff. It's safe to say that she was most definitely a big fan.

"I met him once, and he's really, really nice," she gushed, before adding, "Don't you dare put that in the book!" (Sorry, Connie...)

"He *is* a good-looking guy," Erik agreed sagely from the comfort of Gracie's wheelchair.

We started our audio recorders running. This light-hearted banter was meant to keep a positive atmosphere going and maybe add a little energy.

"Do you mind us being in your room, Gracie?" I asked. "Do you like having company?"

Of the many patients who were cared for at Malvern Manor, Gracie's case was one that really tugged at the heart-strings. If there was one particular spirit that I really wanted to make contact with during our stay, it was hers.

"Gracie, Nick was the nice fellow with the beard who spent the night right here in your bed," I went on. "Do you remember him?"

During his night in the room, Nick had left his own recorder running and had picked up the sound of a gruff yell. It was indistinct, but could possibly have been an after-echo of one of Gracie's personalities. Laying there stretched out on her bed, the thought was a little disconcerting.

"Mmmm."

We all looked at one another. None of us had said it. The noise sounded like a person mumbling their agreement, and seemed to have come from the room next door – which was, of course, completely empty.

A pair of old spectacles sat on a shelf next to the bed. According to Josh, they were the only item in the room (short of the wheelchair) that had actually belonged to Gracie herself. There were toys and an assortment of knick-knacks, but these were all much more recent, and had been left by visitors and well-wishers who wanted to leave Gracie a little something to play with.

Connie took the opportunity to put on Gracie's glasses. She sat there quietly, hoping that it would stimulate some sort of response, but the room remained still and calm. There were no repeat *Mmmmms,* and other than the distant sounds of our three fellow investigators walking around upstairs, things remained completely flat.

Apparently Gracie wasn't around, or at least if she was, she didn't seem to be in the mood to interact with us. We spent almost an hour sitting in her room, alternating periods of quietness with chit-chat and casual conversation. Neither approach bore any fruit.

In a way, I was sort of glad that we didn't get anything concrete that could be attributable to Gracie. By all accounts, her life had been a very trying and difficult one – not because she hadn't been well cared for at Malvern

Manor, but because her illness was an extremely challenging condition to deal with. I rather hoped that, instead of lingering in this empty old room of hers after her death, she had moved on to whatever comes after this life. If anybody had earned a little peace and tranquility, it was Gracie.

Many of the documented phenomena that surround her room could just as easily point to a residual haunting as an intelligent one, but there had been a number of interactive EVPs recorded in there, so it seems reasonable to conclude that something at least semi-intelligent sometimes resided there. I was intrigued by the possibility that one or more of her personalities could either have survived the process of bodily death, or alternatively could have left behind a little something of themselves – some form of psychic "echo" or recording – that visitors were sometimes able to play back mentally, when the conditions were right.

The implications for what that meant about the nature of the human soul were potentially staggering. If multiple personalities could exist after death as what we like to call ghosts, spirits, entities, or whatever term is most in vogue among the paranormal community at the moment, it would mean that the form of energy that makes us actually us, is not necessarily one single thing; rather, it would have to be capable of splitting up into multiple entities, each of which could possibly have its own afterlife. I found this idea intriguing, and it only made the fact that we hadn't gotten any kind of result in Gracie's room a little more frustrating and disappointing.

The sound of footsteps on the main staircase told us that our fellow investigators were finished upstairs for now. Gathering up our equipment, Connie, Erik and I went to join them in the break room. It was getting late – or early, depending upon your point of view – and we were all starting to yawn. I checked in on Rosie the haunted doll, who still hadn't deigned to move inside her glass case.

After comparing notes, our consensus was that it was a good time to call it for the night. We still had two more days and nights to spend investigating Malvern Manor, and we wanted to cram in a few hours' sleep before hitting it hard again the next day.

Chapter Thirteen
Barbecue

We surfaced at around eleven o'clock that morning, and made our way straight into Malvern. The rain was absolutely pouring down, so we rushed into the cafe for shelter, and enjoyed a hearty brunch with lots of fortifying coffee for my team-mates, and tea for me.

As we ate and worked on our game plan for the coming day's investigation, one of the waitresses overheard us and asked if we were staying at "the haunted house across the street." When I confirmed that we were, she told us that she had lived and worked in Malvern for many years, and remembered the residents of the Manor very well.

"They were such a nice bunch of people," she said, setting down a glass of ice water. "Very polite and super friendly."

It was a pleasure to hear that she remembered them fondly. Malvern Manor was often the last stop for those people who had nowhere else to go, a safety net for those who would otherwise be abandoned and probably living on the streets. Although much has been made of the claims of abuse that are said to have gone on there, it seems likely that for the vast majority of its lifetime as a care home, those who lived there were treated humanely and cared for as best as possible.

Dashing across the street, we made it out of the downpour and into the relative shelter of the car port. Erik was the official keeper of the keys. He unlocked the back door and let us all inside. Stephen made straight for the heating vent, stretching out his arms to warm up his cold hands.

I checked in on Rose the haunted doll, who was stubbornly in the exact same position we had left her in earlier that morning. A quick walk-around of the building told us that nothing was noticeably out of place.

We agreed to start out on the second floor, randomly choosing one of the rooms we hadn't hit yet – Room 24. This was right in the area of the Captain's Corner, and was also home to a web-cam that was streaming footage over the Internet on a 24/7 basis.

Stephen hooked up his Geoport ITC box and sat down on his plastic bucket, then began asking the spirits of the Manor to speak. Stephen is a big fan of the device. Personally, while I had seen some fascinating results come from it on more than one occasion, I thought that the reverb effect also made it very prone to false positives because of the high probability of audio pareidolia.

Calling out to any entities that might be present, we were rewarded with a constant stream of what I'm pretty sure was nothing more than gibberish.

"I would really, really like to talk to Gracie," Stephen said, full of optimism. "How many personalities did Gracie have?"

The response sounded somewhat like, *A few,* though the clarity was far from conclusive.

"How many personalities specifically, though?" Jill challenged it.

Nine.

If indeed we really had heard the word *nine,* then that was an interesting number indeed because it was significantly lower than the commonly-stated figure of thirteen. Of course, it is entirely possible that our brains were misinterpreting random noise emanating from the speaker as being meaningful information.

Fortunately, the next response was a lot clearer and unequivocal.

"What did we eat last night that was

so...disagreeable?" Stephen asked.

BARBECUE, boomed the Geoport.

We collapsed in fits of laughter. The voice was absolutely correct. We had chosen a barbecue joint that I won't name (it isn't in Malvern) for our evening meal, and while the food had been good and hearty fare at the time, it had turned the corridors of Malvern Manor into a pungent, fart-infested maze that had taken hours to die down.

Once the laughter had subsided, Jill asked the box to name some of the people present in the room. What sounded like *Hi, Stephen,* came through, and when she indicated me and asked what my name was, the reply came through immediately: *Richard.*

Geoports and similar 'ghost box'-type devices have always fascinated me. Just how much of this was real, and how much could be put down to audio pareidolia? We are all effectively 'wired' to hear the sound of our own name being spoken, after all, so could the Geoport simply be putting out random gibberish, and we in turn were then imposing our own false mental patterns upon those meaningless sounds?

The answer is yes, that is absolutely a possibility. Having been there in person and heard it with my own ears, however, even if I discount what sounded like our names being spoken, that still leaves a very clear (and to my mind, impressive) enunciation of the word *barbecue*, which also happened to be a direct answer to a question that had just been asked...and a correct answer, at that. Audio pareidolia and mere coincidence, on the one hand – or meaningful communication with a discarnate entity of some kind, on the other? To this day, I am not entirely sure myself.

"What about Johnny Houser?" I asked, remembering Johnny's apparent connection with the house. "Is Johnny going to come and visit?"

Hope so, the Geoport responded immediately.

For the next few minutes, try as we might, nothing but garbage spewed out of the box. Although some of my fellow investigators believed that they heard certain words or phrases interpolated with the morass of noise, I personally couldn't make out anything remotely meaningful. Stephen finally conceded defeat (though we were all very happy with the barbecue response) and decided to pack up the Geoport box and try something else instead.

There was an interesting coda to this particular story, however. During the evidence review phase, we discovered that after Stephen had asked whether Suzie was anywhere in the vicinity, what sounded like a faint but definitely discernible giggle was recorded. Judging from the sound level, whoever had spoken (and there were no other people than us in the Manor) would have had to have been outside the room and further down the corridor...probably in the area of Suzie's room.

"It almost sounds like a child playing," Jill said what we were all thinking when we reviewed the clip. That would fit with the experiences reported by numerous other visitors – a little girl, believed to be Inez, was said to run up and down the corridor, laughing, giggling, and sometimes even calling out her name and asking for somebody to come and play with her. That particular hallway would definitely need watching.

Chapter Fourteen
An Ax Murder Connection

It was a dark and stormy night...

So many old-time ghost stories begin like that. As the sun set on Malvern Manor for our third night there, storm clouds gathered over the building, dark and swollen. The heavens opened, dumping an impressive amount of rain on the roof. It had been our intention to head up to the attic next for another EVP session, but the constant *rat-a-tat-tat* of fat raindrops on the roof made working up there nigh-on impossible, so we changed tack and decided to relocate to Hank's room instead.

A low rumble announced the thunder's arrival. Now it really felt like we were in a horror movie. I couldn't help but wonder whether the extra ionization in the air would contribute to the level of paranormal activity over the coming night. We certainly hoped so.

Jill made herself busy going through the chest of drawers, slowly removing articles of clothing one by one and folding them with exaggerated motions. "Hank, I'm folding your clothes," she called out, practically daring Hank to try and stop her. We were hoping that his general dislike for females and his specific distaste for having strangers touch his clothing would coax him out of the woodwork to interact with us.

It's important to point out that Jill was being very respectful as she folded the clothes neatly and carefully, replacing them back in the drawer when she was done. Her intent wasn't to provoke or taunt, but rather to stimulate some kind of response.

Eric held up a pair of shoes. "Lost soles," he deadpanned, eliciting a groan from the rest of us.

Stephen held up a tiny shoe. "I just found the sole of a child."

More groans. It was too early for us to be getting this punchy. Believe it or not, we're a very professional bunch of investigators, by and large, but we don't like to let things get too serious. We all have a fairly juvenile sense of humor. Spending days on end inside cold and abandoned buildings would be pretty miserable without it. Joking around is great for keeping morale up.

Hank didn't seem to want to respond to Jill's impromptu folding. Stephen fired up the Geoport again and immediately began getting results.

Bastard, the box said in a gravelly male voice, followed almost immediately by, *Hank's room.*

"Is Hank here?" I asked.

No.

"What's your name?" Stephen asked. The response was immediate, loud, and extremely clear: *Henry.*

I wasn't buying that this was audio pareidolia. Henry was, of course, Hank's proper, given name, and had been said in direct response to a question.

"Henry, are these your clothes?" I wanted to know.

Yes.

It was interesting to note that the voice that now answered had completely changed, sounding more like that of a young child than an older male. Once again I was forced to wonder whether we were genuinely dealing with the spirit of a child, or if something else was deliberately masquerading as one for its own amusement.

Houser, the box said again, and then repeated itself: *Houser.*

We all looked at one another. There was that Johnny Houser link again.

Henry.

The quality of the voices began to deteriorate, so

Stephen elected to end the session. "Say goodnight, Henry."

Goodnight, boss.

Well, that certainly told us.

"Goodnight, Henry," Jill said. "Don't worry, we'll be back..."

We filed out into the corridor. It was now freezing cold inside the Manor, which was, with the exception of our break room, totally unheated. It felt *so* good to get back to that sanctuary of warmth. Filling up the electric kettle, Stephen graciously made us each a hot cup of tea while we discussed our next move.

"Remember how the name 'Johnny Houser' kept coming through Nick and Katrina's ITC device," Erik mused. "And now we just got the name *Houser* through Stephen's Geoport. I wonder why he keeps turning up in connection with this place. I mean, he's best known as the Villisca Ax Murder House guy."

"He's been to Malvern Manor a few times though," I pointed out, remembering what Josh had told us about Johnny's encounter with the Shadow Man. "Johnny's a Facebook friend of mine. Shall I try and get him over here?"

It turned out that Johnny was too busy to join us for the weekend. When I called him on the phone, he was sitting downstairs in the Villisca Ax Murder House, waiting for the latest crop of visitors who had chartered the house for the night to arrive. "I've got some time to kill before they get here," Johnny said, which probably wasn't the best choice of words, considering the nature of his location. "Want me to see if I can stir something up for you guys?"

That was exactly what I'd been hoping for. Stephen, Jill, Connie, Susan, Erik and I went back over to the nursing home wing. I set my phone down in roughly the same spot where Johnny had been standing when he'd had his encounter with the Shadow Man. Cranking up the volume and switching on the speaker-phone, I stepped back.

We asked Johnny about his connection with Malvern Manor. He acknowledged that he was somehow drawn to the place, but couldn't for the life of him say why that might be. Then Johnny asked how things were going. Erik and Jill recounted their experience of the night before, when some kind of dark entity had pursued them along the second floor hallway and down the main staircase.

"Last time I was here with Dustin [Pari] I felt some serious negative energy in that area too," he told us. "I felt like I was going to throw up and pass out. I nearly had a full-blown panic attack in that same spot, right near the Captain's

Corner."

That was an interesting piece of corroborative testimony, so far as I was concerned. An almost identical experience in the same location, experienced by two parties who had never met, let alone exchanged information.

"Tell us about your experience with the Shadow Man," I asked. Josh had already told us the story, but I wanted to hear it straight from the horse's mouth, so to speak.

"It was dusk, just getting dark outside," Johnny began. "It was a little later than it is right now. I was standing in the hallway with the curtain at the end."

"We're looking at it right now."

"There was a dark shape at the end of that corridor. It was darker than dark, if that makes any sense. I looked away and looked back, trying to figure out if my eyes were playing tricks. Then I crouched down to get a better look...and it came right at me."

"How would you describe it?"

"I call it a 'Shadow Man,' but it was...part man, part black mass. It had a definite shape, but it was unfinished somehow. It was the first time that I've ever had a shadow figure run at me. Usually they disappear as soon as you see them. I stared at this thing for a good thirty seconds before it ran at me."

"Did you pick up on any sense of intelligence or intent?"

"It was such a rush, a 'holy crap, that just happened!' It felt familiar, almost as if it knew who and what I was. Definitely didn't feel as if it was a stranger. It was freaky, scary, and downright odd. I felt like this thing somehow knew me."

We paused for a minute to digest that. All of us were looking at the end of the Shadow Man's hallway, keeping a watchful eye on the door of Room 2. The feeling of a spirit entity of some kind knowing things about you individually, taking a personal interest in you, had to be a terrifying one, and I could only imagine how Johnny must have felt at the time.

It was clear that he had put a lot of thought into what exactly the link between himself and Malvern Manor might be, and now he advanced a truly intriguing theory. The murders at Villisca had been brutal and savage beyond imagination, yet the perpetrator had never been identified, let alone caught and brought to justice. Some have speculated that the killer was in fact a drifter, a hobo that aimlessly rode the railroad tracks throughout Iowa and the surrounding states, which would explain how he managed to elude capture after the bloody deed was done.

It is well-known that the hotel which would one day become Malvern Manor was constructed with the express purpose of servicing travelers on the railroad, primarily businessmen and others who were passing through on their journey to faraway places. Could the Villisca murderer have spent the night at Malvern Manor either before or after carrying out his night of butchery? When one thought about it, it was entirely plausible.

"Newspapers at the time of the murder actually said that 'the Devil himself got off the train at Villisca that night,'" Johnny said, "which is pretty darn creepy when you stop to think about it."

"So is it possible that either the Shadow Man or some other entity here knows you because it has been to Villisca itself?" I asked.

"It very well might. It has always been my belief that if somebody who does what we do – by which I mean, paranormal investigators – catches a glimpse of one of them, then they somehow get to know us right back."

That particular thought sent a cold chill running

straight down my spine, and it was nothing to do with how frigid the air was becoming in the nursing home wing. Johnny had just given voice to a belief that was very common among members of the paranormal interest community – that if you took too much of an interest in the other world, then the chances were good that it would start taking an interest right back if you weren't very careful about it. The implications of that weren't very comforting, to say the least.

"I've also been told that there may also be a geological component to this," Johnny went on, "in the form of a huge line of quartz that is said to run between Malvern and Villisca. I haven't been able to verify or disprove this yet, but it's something I'm looking into."

Johnny was referring to another fairly widespread theory, one which holds that certain types of rocks and minerals may be implicated in increased levels of paranormal activity. Geologists tend to laugh at the idea, but it has nonetheless gained a great deal of credence among those who are engaged in the study of paranormal phenomena. If what Johnny has heard about the quartz vein is true – and I am by no means claiming that it is – then it would indeed turn out to be a tangible link between two extremely haunted locations.

"Okay, enough of the theory. Let's see if I can stir some stuff up for ya." Johnny cleared his throat. He raised his voice. "So, spirits of Malvern Manor...this is Johnny Houser. I've got some friends that are staying there tonight. They'd love to communicate with you. Now, you know me. You ran right at me."

A knock sounded from somewhere further down the hallway. Jill went to get a better look, but found nothing to explain it. The downpour had ended outside, and the wind had dropped back to little more than a very light breeze. Whatever had made that sound, it sure seemed to be right there inside the nursing home wing with us. When I asked Jill where the noise had originated from, she wordlessly pointed toward one of the old patient rooms. I went inside, shining my flashlight beam around the walls, checking underneath the bed and inside the closets. Nothing. The room was utterly empty.

"You don't need to play this cat and mouse game you're so fond of," Johnny went on. "Don't play games with these guys. They came a long way to see you, so please let yourselves be seen. Go right up to 'em and give 'em some epic evidence, huh?

"If you have something to do with Villisca, well, I'm sitting here at the Villisca Ax Murder House right now. Were you a living being at one point in time, or are you some sort of entity that was never human, that never lived a physical life? We just want to know who you are and what you are."

He paused, letting things go quiet. Nothing moved in the hallway. The only sound was that of the six of us breathing. I looked around, scanning from doorway to doorway. My eyes had adapted to the dark about as well as they were going to. I was hoping to catch sight of one of the shadow figures Josh had warned us about, but so far, nothing.

"Please give us some kind of sound, some kind of sign," Johnny said. "Let us know that you're here."

Aside from the rumbling of somebody's stomach, nothing stirred.

"I hate to say it, but I think this is a bust," I said finally. My colleagues agreed. Reluctant to give up on the Shadow Man's hallway, we nonetheless decided to cut our losses and relocate to the second floor in the vicinity of the Captain's Corner. Hopefully we'd have better luck up there.

We went straight to Hank's room, reasoning that

because this was where we had gotten the name *Houser* several times through the Geoport, we might get results by bringing in the man himself, even if he was at the other end of a phone line rather than being present in the flesh. Johnny was still willing to give it his best shot.

"Hank, buddy, what's going on? My friends there tell me you were talking about me earlier tonight. What is it that you want? What can I do for you?" Remembering that Hank was known for being somewhat cranky, sitting on the porch and throwing stones at passing children, Johnny invited him to throw a few stones at us if he felt like it. "When I was here with Nick and Katrina, we felt your presence up there. You don't have to hide. We all know you're here."

The floor creaked slightly as we shifted our weight. None of our instruments were registering anything out the ordinary; EMF and temperature levels were all normal. A car drove by in the street outside.

"What I really want to know, Hank, is this...is there a link between Malvern Manor and the Villisca Ax Murder House. Because I'm sitting in that house right now, and— wow." The phone went silent for a second. When Johnny's voice returned, he told us that he had just heard knocking above him, up on the second floor of what he called the Ax

House.

Something was apparently trying to make its presence known. Whoever or whatever it was, seemed to be eavesdropping in on Johnny's end of the conversation.

"Johnny, please confirm that there's absolutely *nobody* else in that house with you," I asked.

"Absolutely nobody here but me, sitting all on my own downstairs. I've been over the house when I arrived. It's empty."

As quickly as it had begun, the knocking stopped. It had been clear and distinct, but of a very short duration, almost as if an invisible interloper had wanted to announce its presence, and then slink back into the woodwork once more. Try as he might, Johnny could not get anything to happen in Hank's room.

We relocated to the hallway outside Inez's room. Before signing off for the night, Johnny invited any spirits that might be present to use the energy from our cameras, equipment, and even our bodies in order to help manifest some paranormal activity later that night. He closed with a personal message to Inez, telling her that she could trust us, and strongly encouraged her to come out and play with us.

Erik mentioned that we had heard and recorded

what sounded like a child giggling or playing in this very same spot just a few hours earlier.

"That reminds me of what happened just a couple of weeks ago," Johnny said. "We were using an Echo Box up here, and got something so weird – it sounded like a conversation between a couple of little kids, right in the place where you're standing now."

Aware that he had other commitments, I thanked him for his time and asked his advice on where best we might concentrate our time and attention during the night's investigation.

"I recommend you focus your attention on the hallway leading to Inez's room and the attic," he replied after a thoughtful pause. "Something almost felt like it was laying in wait to ambush Nick and I last time we were both there for *Paranormal Lockdown.* It was right after we'd experimented with infrasound.

"Here's my parting shot for the night: It's so hard to get a handle on that place. You've got so many different dynamics happening all at once. Inez, the little girl – of course, you don't want to be mean to a little kid. Then you've got Hank, the grumpy old man. Sometimes, in my opinion, you've got to be a little grumpy right back at him in order to get a little respect back from him, you know?" I nodded in agreement, which was pretty silly because it wasn't as though Johnny could see me. "Then you have the factor of mental illness. There's a lot of confusion going on in that place. I advise you to throw out a lot of different techniques. Sooner or later, something's going to hit a nerve."

"What about Gracie's room?"

"A lot of confusion in there too. It's almost like some of the mental challenges she suffered in life are still active in there today. It can be pretty overwhelming in there at times. Be sure to stay respectful."

We thanked Johnny for graciously agreeing to assist us with our investigation. Hanging up, I slipped the phone back into my pocket. My hand stayed there. It was getting to be so cold that my teeth wanted to start chattering.

"What next?" Stephen asked.

I grinned. "Well, I don't know about you, but I could *murder* a cup of tea…"

Chapter Fifteen
Get Out

After Johnny Houser had so graciously taken the time to phone in and try to stir up a little activity, we all agreed that it was time to strike while the iron was hot. Picking up a selection of equipment, we headed over to the nursing wing to conduct another spirit box session, using an Ovilus and several digital voice recorders.

Putting down our upended plastic buckets to use as seats in the center of the corridor, the six of us began laughing and joking, trying to lighten up the atmosphere as much as we could. The humor was pretty juvenile, even by our admittedly low standards, and after Stephen made a spectacularly crude joke, Erik heard the sound of a woman laughing coming from the direction of Room 7.

Naturally, there was nobody to be found at the far end of the hallway. As Erik had been the only one to hear the sound, and a replay of the audio files didn't pick anything up, we were going to have to throw this out as debunked – or at the very least, completely subjective, which is essentially the same thing. Anecdote doesn't count as evidence.

If this was a ghost-hunting TV show or a Hollywood movie, stuff would have been flying around the hallways and bouncing off the walls by now. With this being reality, however, we spent over an hour in the dark hallway trying to get somebody – anybody, we really weren't fussy – to interact with us. Our efforts were in vain. No Shadow Man appeared outside Room 2 to charge at us; no lady screamed from within the confines of Room 7.

These are the moments when the energy levels start to flag, and if you aren't careful, it's easy to get disheartened. Paranormal field research is almost always a feast or famine affair, and in my experience the famine part of it is by far the most common – anywhere from eighty to ninety percent of your time is spent waiting around for the remaining ten to twenty percent. That time isn't wasted; it's more a case of delayed gratification, the price that you pay in order to experience something genuinely inexplicable. It really helps to be in the company of good friends, which helps the time pass more quickly, even if nothing remotely paranormal happens at all.

Ask any experienced paranormal investigator and they'll tell you that it's when your expectations are low and you let your guard down, even just a little, that the unexpected pops us and smacks you right between the eyes. Picking up our buckets and equipment, we made our way back to the break room. Unbeknownst to her, Jill hadn't switched off the Ovilus, which spoke words in the voice of *Beyond the Darkness* podcast host Dave Schrader.

Just as we were walking past Grace's room, Jill called out a cheery, "Hi, Gracie!"

Grace.

The voice was a familiar one – our friend Dave had just spoken via the Ovilus speaker. That stopped Jill dead in her tracks. The name 'Grace' was one of thousands of words stored in the Ovilus database, and it was a word that hadn't come through the box at all over the past few days. It has become a personal maxim that the field of paranormal investigation has long since stretched my willingness to believe in coincidence to breaking point, and Jill's experience was a textbook illustration of why that was the case: what was the likelihood that the Ovilus was suddenly hit upon the word 'Grace' at the precise instant that Jill happened to say it out loud...and as she was walking past the doorway to Gracie's room? The odds against that happening had to be nothing short of astronomical.

The message was pretty clear to us all: our next

target location ought to be Gracie's room.

Deciding to take the advice given by the Ovilus, our entire group relocated to Gracie's room for an EVP session. The six of us were in fine spirits, and though it was a fairly small room, we each managed to fit ourselves in there comfortably.

Connie found herself drawn to the pair of spectacles that lay on a small shelf next to the bed. Josh had told us that the glasses had actually belonged to Gracie herself. It took minimal urging to convince Connie to try them on. Slipping them carefully over her ears, she blinked a few times as her eyes adjusted to the lenses.

Stephen fired up the spirit box, which immediately began to spit out its usual stream of gibberish. He made sure that the device was not set to receive external radio signals. Some spirit box apps intentionally use radio waves or IP radio as an audio source, which adds a degree of contamination to the final output, in my opinion – though the results can be excellent sometimes.

So far as I was concerned, the atmosphere in Gracie's room was relaxed and casual, nothing like the sense of heavy oppression that many visitors had reported experiencing in there. Stephen, on the other hand, found it to be entirely different.

"It's thick in here," he grimaced. "It's hard to describe, but there are...reverberations of many personalities here. Echoes, if you like. I spent half an hour in here earlier, and the feeling was really strong then. It's almost as if those energies seeped into the walls somehow."

We were suddenly interrupted by the spirit box.

MALVERN, said a voice through the speaker. It was extremely clear, and despite being just a single word, the specificity of it was very impressive. The tone of voice had sounded a little sinister to me, but many of the voices coming through the spirit box can.

The next sentence spoken was just two words, but they definitely weren't friendly:

Get out.

I'll be the first to admit that "Get out" is a Hollywood horror cliche, thanks to The Amityville Horror and countless other scary movies, but there it was, coming through the spirit box loud and clear.

"We're not getting out," Susan said, in a tone that brooked no disagreement.

Evil, the box said next, and then repeated the same word again.

Stephen attempted to contact Gracie herself, but received nothing in the way of an intelligible response. Because we don't know for sure what ultimately happened to her (she may even have been alive and living in another facility, for all that we knew) there was no guarantee whatsoever that whoever or whatever was active in that room was anything to do with Gracie herself. Stephen was convinced that remnants of several of her personalities could still be felt there, but even if that truly were the case, those energies could just as easily have been residual recordings rather than actual intelligent entities that were capable of communication.

Once again, we found ourselves pondering the question of whether multiple distinct personalities could survive death in the same way that a single human personality seems to be able to. When we talk about a human spirit entity, we are generally referring to the energy of a single individual – their spirit, soul, life essence, call it what you will; but if a person has multiple personalties, do they all stem from the same spirit or soul, in the same way that a diamond has many different facets but is still one single stone? Or was it possible that each of those personalities survived as its own quasi-intelligent entity, independent of all of the others? If so, that raised some fascinating questions about the nature of the human soul.

At the end of our EVP session, we had come out with more questions than answers. We discussed the metaphysical implications of Gracie's unique case as we picked up our equipment.

"Where the heck did my TASCAM go?" Stephen asked, sounding rather annoyed. He had set down his audio recorder on the shelf from which Connie had taken Gracie's glasses. Now it was gone. "It was right here," he grumbled. "I set it down in the middle of the shelf."

We all began looking around, starting with the floor in case it had somehow dropped – unlikely, as we would have heard the impact. Hunting high and low, Stephen finally found the TASCAM inside the burlap bag that he had brought along with him. The bag was hanging from one of the handles of the wheelchair which occupied a corner of Gracie's room, about three feet away from where Stephen had carefully set the recorder down.

"You must have put it in there yourself without thinking about it," I reasoned, attempting to debunk it.

"We're all at that forgetful age, mate – you know, the one where you walk into a room and forget why you went in there in the first place. Even if it's the toilet."

"I know for sure that I didn't," Stephen insisted, before adding that one of the five of us would almost certainly have noticed him moving the recorder, particularly as it was still switched on.

Cat and mouse.

Josh's words came back to me yet again. Something was most definitely playing games with us. Now the big question was, was the spirit box telling us the truth when it said the word, Evil? Or was it just another of Malvern Manor's ghostly pranksters having a laugh at our expense?

Only time would tell.

Chapter Sixteen
Glass Work

We headed upstairs to check out some odd noises on the second floor. As soon as we reached the top of the stairs, Jill was immediately on edge, telling us that the dark energy which had pursued her and Erik down the stairs the night before was still lurking up here, and was definitely not pleased to see us.

"It's right behind us," she insisted, peering into the darkness just beyond the Captain's Corner.

"Don't give us any bloody attitude tonight," I growled, sounding a lot braver than I actually felt.

We made a sweep around, checking all the rooms, and finding nothing out of place, we went on with our next experiment: a glass divination session in the kitchen. Whatever it was that liked to hang out upstairs could wait until later.

Glass divination is an old technique used for spirit communication. It is simple and easy to perform, requiring only a smooth, flat surface such as a tabletop, and a glass or a cup. Well, I say 'glass' but even plastic cups will work. The participants all gather around the surface and each place a fingertip lightly on the base of the upended glass, which then has to be opened up for communication with a statement of intent. A typical example goes something like this:

"We are opening up this glass as a means of spirit communication. Only spirits with good and benevolent intentions are permitted to use it; no dark or negative energies are allowed to come through."

Ideally, the glass will begin to move about the table, usually in a circular pattern. Yes/no questions can then be asked of it. Skeptics state that the glass is being moved by the sitters themselves, albeit subconsciously, using ideomotor activity – a way in which muscles can operate without being deliberately told to do so. Believers, on the other hand, assert that spirits are able to guide the glass by using the energy of the participants, which is transmitted by using their fingertips as a sort of energy conduit.

As with so many techniques used for paranormal investigation, I am on the fence about glass divination. On the one hand, I have seen it yield some highly specific results (I'll never forget the times when the glass gave correct answers to questions that none of the participants could possibly have known) but on the other, ideomotor activity and the human subconscious are very real forces, and certainly there are some instances in which the glass is being influenced by one or more of those who have their fingertips on it. In my view, it's just like any other tool – it has its place, but your individual mileage will vary. If you like it, and it works for you, then use it; if not, don't. It's really as simple as that.

Stephen, Connie, and I were the first participants. The kitchen counter-top was the perfect surface for it. We were using a plastic Mos Eisley Cantina cup that I'd picked up at Star Wars Celebration the year before – my inner nerd was showing.

"Have any of the spirits here ever done this before?" Stephen asked. "Do you know how to move this glass, using our energy to do so?"

Outside, the rainfall was getting heavier, drumming against the roof and walls of the Manor.

After a while (and a few changes of participants) the cup finally began to move, slowly at first, but quickly gaining momentum. Jill, Connie, and I seemed to be an acceptable combination; the cup moved toward Jill and Connie immediately upon request, but flatly refused to move toward me, no matter how much I cajoled, so I gave up my spot to Stephen.

I must have been acting as some kind of brake, because when the priest replaced me at the counter-top, the cup began to positively fly. Susan established a simple means of communication that utilized a clockwise rotation for "yes" and anti-clockwise for "no."

The cup seemed to respond best to Connie's questioning (when asked "do you like Connie?" the answer was a definite yes. Susan was also popular. Assuming that what followed was a genuine case of spirit communication, as opposed to the unintentional manipulation of the cup by the sitters' own subconsciouses, a fascinating story began to unfold. The communicator claimed to be a female nurse, one who would not accept that she might be dead; she said that she had worked at Malvern Manor and been very happy during her time there.

The nurse was apparently still taking care of her charges, despite the fact that there had been no residents for quite a few years.

It's appropriate to be somewhat skeptical of the results obtained through any technique of purported spirit communication, so I decided to put our phantom nurse to the test – with her permission, of course. I explained that Erik, who was currently standing in the corner of the room and not physically touching the cup, was going to hold up a number of fingers behind his back. Would the spirit be willing to tell us how many fingers he was holding up?

The cup circled clockwise to indicate that it would.

"Is Erik holding up five fingers?" I asked. After a few seconds' hesitation, the cup circled in an anti-clockwise direction.

"Is Erik holding up four fingers?" This time, the response was an immediate and very deliberate *no.*

"Three fingers?"

Yes.

All five of us looked at Erik expectantly. After letting us hang on tenterhooks for a few seconds, he slowly raised his hand. The middle three fingers were held straight up.

We could only conclude that the participants had somehow made a lucky guess (a one in five chance), Erik was committing an act of fraud (something he has never done before to my knowledge, as he is a man of great integrity)...or we were dealing with a genuine case of communication with some sort of discarnate entity.

Personally, I was leaning toward the latter

explanation.

Thanking the spirit entity (which claimed to be named "Sally,") we got down to the business of asking the nurse a few more questions. Erik and Jill stayed off the cup at first, while Stephen, Connie, Susan and I participated. The answers soon indicated that the nurse wanted all six of us to participate at the same time. It was a bit of a squeeze, but we managed to make it work after cosying up to one another.

"Are you willing to knock or make a noise somewhere in the Manor?" I asked.

NO.

The spirit had apparently had enough of being tested for one night. She claimed to have worked at the Manor sometime during the 1960s. Connie asked her if her name was 'Sally,' to which the answer was yes. Sally was a name that had come through several times upstairs on the Spectreceiver voice box. Sally said that she had worked at Malvern Manor for several years but had passed away long before it closed for the last time. (Without having access to personnel records from the 1960s, it is impossible to confirm whether this claim is true or not).

"Do you see any other spirits here beside you?" Stephen asked.

Yes.

"Are they friendly?" I asked.

Yes.

"Do you like Josh?"

Yes.

Connie asked whether the spirit liked us, and was given an affirmative answer. That was nice to hear. Sally went on to say that the residential facility was a very friendly place to live and work at during her tenure. She said that she remained at Malvern Manor intentionally, as she believed that there were still patients to be looked over and protected.

"Are there any spirits here that mean the patients harm?" Susan asked. The answer was *No,* but when I asked whether there were any entities haunting the place that meant our team of investigators harm, the cup indicated a very strong *Yes.* That might be cause for a little apprehension, I thought, remembering the experience that Jill and Erik had on the second floor and the main staircase.

Susan enquired whether some of those spirits were up on the second floor *(yes)* but when she asked whether ALL of those malicious entities were up there, the answer was no – some were on the ground floor with us, and others were up in the attic.

I asked whether Sally knew Johnny Houser *(yes)* and liked him *(yes)*. "Did you hear us talking to Johnny earlier?"

The cup shot clockwise around the counter-top as though it was rocket-propelled, one of the strongest affirmative responses that we had gotten all night.

"Is there some kind of link between the Villisca Ax Murder House where Johnny hangs out, and Malvern Manor?" Susan wanted to know. An extremely strong *yes* that we had a challenge stopping.

"Is it a quartz line?" Stephen interjected.

Yes.

Then I decided to ask the question that had been at the back of my mind ever since my conversation with Johnny: Had the person (or persons, depending on whichever theory you believed) who committed the Villisca murders ever come to Malvern Manor?

YES.

"Is the spirit of that murderer still around now, in this building?"

Yes.

"Does the Villisca murderer go back to the house where he killed that poor family?" Susan asked.

No.

A loud thud from upstairs made us all look toward the ceiling. That was exactly what had happened to Johnny when he was chatting to us while inside the Villisca Ax Murder House, which was quite the coincidence – if you believe in such things as coincidences.

"Is the Villisca murderer here tonight?"

Yes.

I'd be lying if I said that wasn't a little bit creepy. Things had suddenly taken a turn toward the Hollywood. Were we really in the company of a psychopathic, homicidal entity? If so, the prospect was a rather disconcerting one, to say the least.

Sticking to the same line of questioning, Stephen asked whether the murderer had committed other, similar crimes. The answer was once again, *Yes.* That dovetailed neatly with the commonly-held theory that the Villisca murderer had been responsible for other equally brutal massacres, such as the case in Colorado Springs in which two families in neighboring houses were butchered while asleep in their beds – just as the family at Villisca had been.

"Was one of those families also in Kansas?"

Yes.

Stephen was very much satisfied with the answers

we had gotten. Susan asked Sally whether she was at peace, and was happy to be told that indeed she was. She was told that there were other good-natured spirits here that acted as protectors for those who were weaker, and that one such ghost was that of Captain Cullers. The Captain gets a bad rap sometimes, and hearing that he was serving as a sort of "guardian angel" made me wonder whether he might have been misunderstood.

"Is the Captain a nice man?"

NO.

Hmmm. Definitely not the answer I had been expecting, but then again, life is replete with examples of those who do good deeds without being particularly nice individuals. Why should Captain Cullers be any different?

Sally told us that he wasn't actually there in the Manor with us that night, which was a bit of a disappointment, and then went on to say that he had not been the dark entity that had pursued Erik and Jill from the second floor down to the bottom of the staircase. Whatever the unpleasant energy was that haunted the second floor, it was something other than the spirit of Captain Cullers.

The obvious next question was to ask whether there were any inhuman entities present. The answer was a very fast, *Yes.* Susan received the same answer when she asked whether a spirit had come along as an attachment to the doll, Rosie.

"Does that spirit refer to itself as 'Number Two?'" Susan asked, deliberately getting the name wrong. The glass responded in the negative.

"Does it go by the name of 'Number One?'" asked Jill. This time, the answer was a vigorous, *YES.* We were so impressed that none of us even thought to make any Number Two jokes. "Was the spirit that chased Erik and I downstairs human?"

NO.

Well, that destroyed the "maybe it was Captain Cullers" theory.

Susan declared that we had all established our own forms of spiritual protection prior to entering the Manor, and asked whether those preparations had been adequate. We were all relieved when the glass answered in the affirmative, particularly when the answer to my next question – was the entity capable of hurting any of our team – came back as a very strong *YES.*

With that, we ended our session and closed down the glass as a means of spirit communication. That was certainly food for thought. We would do well to stay on our guard as the investigation went on. That was something for us to bear in mind the following day. Right now, it was getting on for sunrise. The team was starting to get tired and our beds were calling.

Chapter Seventeen

Footsteps in the Dark

Saturday was to be our last night spent investigating at Malvern Manor. We also hoped that it would be our best. After a hearty brunch in the busy cafe (it was St. Patrick's Day, and some of the revelers were starting their celebrations early) we went over to the Manor a little before 2pm.

After her experience with the dark energy form on the staircase, Jill wasn't in the mood to take any crap this time. She decided to lay down the law right out of the gate. With a determined spring in her step, she made straight for the main staircase, holding a voice recorder in her left hand.

"What do you want?" Jill demanded of the empty air. "I'm here to let you know that I know you're here. You've made your presence known. I don't like the fact that you're crowding my space. You need to back off. I'm not here to mess with you, so don't you mess with me...okay? Can we agree on that?"

Satisfied that she had made her point, Jill came downstairs and returned to the break room. We hooked her voice recorder into an external speaker and played back her verbal ultimatum. No sooner had she said, "Can we agree on that?" than a voice, meek and childlike, responded with the word, *Yes.*

"There it is," a jubilant Stephen said. "You got your answer."

Jill played the recording back several times in order to make sure that it did indeed say what we thought it did. It sounded as if something up on the second floor was agreeing with her. The question was, was this truly the dark entity that had pursued Jill and Erik down the staircase, or perhaps one of the other spirits that haunted the second floor, such as Inez or Suzie?

Stephen, Jill, and Erik wanted to try and recreate the extraordinary SLS camera footage that they had gotten in Inez's room the year before. I had reviewed the footage prior to visiting, and had found it to be fascinating. It looked as if a small figure was hanging from the top of the closet, and then a second figure appeared to be trying to pull it down. When the hanging figure fell, a voice came through their spirit box saying "She's down." (I encourage the reader to form their own judgment by visiting this link: http://www.ghostpi.com/malvern.html)

All six of us filed into the hallway outside Inez's room, while the three AAPI investigators set to work with the SLS. Stephen fired up the spirit box once more. After only ten seconds had passed, it said the word, *Villisca.*

The investigators began calling out to any spirit entities that might be present, inviting them to come forward and speak. When nothing intelligible came through the speaker, Jill and Stephen tried specific names, some of which had come through the spirit box earlier during our investigation, and others which were associated with the building; names such as Inez, Otto, Suzie, and Sally.

I was a little disappointed to find that as time went on, they seemed to be having no luck. Operating the SLS, Jill picked up on what appeared to be a figure, but it seemed more as if it was the software attempting to make sense of the straight edges of the doorframe, rather than being something truly anomalous. After the initial excitement of hearing the word *Villisca*, the remainder of the session was ultimately fruitless. We had gotten better results with the SLS when we were pursuing the stick figure along the second floor hallway earlier in the investigation. That's just the way the cookie crumbles when it comes to paranormal investigation: Nobody gets consistently good results every time, no matter how haunted the location or what tools and talents they use...and despite what you may have seen on TV.

Stephen decided to conduct a solo Spectreceiver session in the parlor with the rest of us were doing other things. After a while, Erik and I went to check on him. We hung out for a while, listening to what sounded like meaningless chatter come through the speaker. Satisfied that not much was happening, we left.

It was only afterward that we would learn that as soon as we were out of the room, Stephen had asked, "Who just left?" Almost immediately, a deep, gravelly male voice answered with: *Richard.*

The sound was as much a growl as it was a spoken word, but it certainly did sound like my name had been spoken. As to whether this was a true case of EVP or simply audio pareidolia, I find it difficult to objectively say. We are all biased toward hearing the sound of our own names being spoken, after all, and once you hear something like that on a recording, it is practically impossible to "un-hear" it. The brain has already wired itself to hear that particular pattern of sounds and inflection. Opinions among the team were divided. Some thought they could hear the word, others thought not. When there's that much doubt about a so-called EVP, we make a habit of throwing it out as possible evidence.

(I would also be lying to you if I said it wasn't at least a little bit creepy. This really wasn't the sort of voice you wanted to hear calling your name.)

On that note, we locked the building up and went to grab some food.

We got back from dinner at a little after eight o'clock. For a small town, Malvern was certainly rocking the St. Paddy's Day spirit. Everywhere we looked was a sea of bright green. People were laughing and having a good time, and unlike in larger towns and cities, we didn't see any signs of aggressive behavior. It did make things a little more challenging in terms of our investigation, however, because sound carries further at night, and the noise of the festivities happening in the town center were audible even inside the Manor. We would just have to put up with the audio contamination for as long as it went on. There was no other choice.

Jill and I decided to check out the atmosphere

upstairs. She was picking up what she could only describe as 'a weird vibe' when we reached the second floor landing, but nothing like what she and Erik had encountered before. It wasn't nearly as strong, for one thing.

We went from room to room, looking inside each one. All was quiet and still...until we hit the doorway of Room 17.

"There it is," Jill breathed. "It's right there, on my back. Tingling, just like the first time we encountered it."

"Don't worry," I said from directly behind her, "I've got your back."

"Nobody's got yours, though," she pointed out mischievously.

I couldn't help but look over my shoulder. All I could see was a dark and seemingly empty hallway.

When we reached the end of the corridor, it became apparent that the attic door was standing wide open.

"We closed that before we left for dinner, right?" I said. Jill agreed that we definitely had. "Is it possible that the thing popped open just because it's an old door in an old frame?"

Wanting to test the theory, we closed the door firmly, making sure that it was securely shut and jiggling the handle for good measure. Then we tried slamming the frame and pounding our shoes on the floorboards in front of it, all in an attempt to get it to spring open.

No dice. It stayed resolutely shut. By experimentation, we found that it took a significant amount of force to open the door.

Jill and I climbed the narrow flight of steps leading up to the attic, just to make sure that we didn't have any flesh and blood visitors. Just as we had expected, there was nobody up there. Closing the door firmly behind us, we headed back in the direction of the main staircase.

"There's something here,' Jill said as we passed the doorways to rooms 17 and 18."I'm not exactly sure what, but there's definitely a presence. It's making the hair stand up on the back of my neck..."

That was all I needed to hear. After going back to the break room and filling in the rest of the team, we all went back to that area to set up some equipment and to conduct a burst EVP session in the hallway between the two rooms.

We asked a few questions, trying to figure out who had opened the attic door in our absence, and also to ascertain the nature of whatever energy Jill had sensed a few moments before. Frustratingly, we got no answers, and Jill reported that she could no longer feel that presence.

Cat and mouse.

"Screw this," Erik said, giving voice to what everyone was thinking. "Does anybody want to see what's happening over on the nursing home wing?"

That sounded like a great idea to us.

It was freezing cold by the time we made it over there. The more sensitive members of the group said that the atmosphere felt very flat to them. In an attempt to liven things up a little, Susan volunteered to do something that quite frankly would never have occurred to me: Bust out some dance moves.

"Who's got some good music?" she asked.

"I don't know about 'good,'" I replied, cranking up the volume on my phone and browsing through my music library, "but this is too good an opportunity to miss."

Which is how the Shadow Man's hallway at Malvern Manor, dark, silent, and haunted, suddenly reverberated to the sounds of *Everything is Awesome* from *The Lego Movie* soundtrack.

"There's no way I'm dancing to that," Susan demurred, insisting on a 'real song.' "Don't you have anything from the 70s?"

"I've got one Bee Gees song. *Stayin' Alive.* I use it for teaching CPR classes."

"Perfect! Cue the music!"

The Brothers Gibb began crooning through the speaker on my phone. Without missing so much as a beat, Susan proceeded to strut her funky stuff, getting on down just a few feet away from the door to Room 2. The only thing missing were a really wide-collared shirt and bell-bottomed slacks.

Speaking as somebody who dances like the middle-aged white man that I am, it was a truly remarkable performance. I was getting tired just watching her throw down some shapes.

"I cannot wait for them to re-enact this on *Haunted Case Files*," I chuckled, referring to the TV show that had covered some of my more intense cases. An impromptu disco boogie in a hallway known to be haunted by a shadow fire was one of the most surreal things I'd ever been a part of.

"If that thing pops out now and starts dancing with her, we're just going to have to retire," said Erik. "I mean, what else could you do after that?"

Unfortunately, the Shadow Man was not inclined to come out and dance.

Nor did it stop with that one particular song; Susan was just getting warmed up. Next came a couple of great tracks from the *Guardians of the Galaxy* movie soundtrack: *Hooked on a Feeling* by Blue Swede, and *Come and Get Your Love* by Redbone.

"If this doesn't stir something up, I doubt anything will," I thought. We finished up with Will Ferrell covering *Afternoon Delight* – because there's always time for a little Ron Burgundy.

None of it worked. When the music stopped and Susan took a few moments to catch her breath, everything was as still and silent as it had been before. Yet again, despite our best efforts, the spirits of Malvern Manor were refusing to play ball.

But all that was about to change.

After another refreshment break, we decided to try a little more glass divination in the kitchen. It was getting close to midnight, and our hope was that things might begin to pick up a little.

This time, the glass sprang to life immediately. Stephen asked whether the female that we were talking to was Sally, and was surprised to hear that she was not. Nor were we communicating with a former nurse or patient;

instead, the unnamed lady claimed to have been employed as a cook at Malvern Manor back in the days when it was a residential facility. That wasn't particularly surprising, given that we were holding our session in the kitchen.

After a few minutes of getting contradictory answers, however, we soon discovered that we were being toyed with.

"Are you being honest with us?" Stephen demanded, to which the glass immediately indicated that it was not. He immediately banished it from the glass, and I stated that we were not willing to work with any spirits whose intentions were dishonorable and that were not going to tell the truth.

Then we started over.

Yet again, the answers we got turned out to be false, leading us on a wild goose chase. Despite our having drawn a line in the sand, whoever (or whatever) was coming through the glass was playing games with us. Frustrated, we shut the glass down and decided to move on to something else.

Things didn't get any better up in the attic. Jill discovered that her camera, which had been fully charged just a short time before, was now completely dead. Unexplained power drains are commonplace at haunted locations, as any paranormal investigator will confirm, and often signals that some kind of activity is about to take place, but in this case the attic was every bit as quiet as the nursing home wing had been. Added to that was the frustration of revelers walking past outside, singing and laughing, injecting their own special brand of noise contamination into our audio recordings.

We were sitting around in the break room, chewing the fat and basically minding our own business, when suddenly there came a loud bang on the back of the chair behind Susan.

It hadn't been Susan shifting position in the chair, and nor was it the sound of the structure settling. This was too loud and distinct for either of those things, a definite impact on the wall itself.

Waiting expectantly for a few more minutes, we were a little disappointed when nothing else out of the ordinary happened. Susan decided that it would be a good idea to be a little more proactive, and so she and I climbed the rickety narrow staircase up to the attic, closing and latching the door behind us.

The gusts of wind had finally died down to a somewhat tolerable level. This was the first time all weekend that the attic wasn't significantly noise-contaminated, and both Susan and I had high hopes for our two-person EVP session. Sadly, our optimism was misplaced; despite its fearsome reputation, we experienced nothing more notable than the sound of an owl hooting. Of the crawling male apparition, there was absolutely no sign. Neither of us felt even remotely nauseated, and as we returned to join the rest of the team, it was with a feeling of slight disappointment.

Our next stop was Hank's room. We made our way inside, standing in a loose circle in the center of the room. Against her better judgment, Connie slipped into one of Hank's flannel shirts (she was the only member of the team small enough for it to fit properly).

Jill asked whether Hank would be kind enough to shut the drawer that Connie had left open. Unsurprisingly, he didn't seem to be willing to oblige. We continued to ask the usual EVP questions, not really expecting much to happen, based upon how quiet the last few hours had been.

The footsteps took us all by surprise. Almost as one, our heads turned to look toward the doorway. They were coming from outside in the corridor.

"Who's out there?" Connie asked. I stuck my head into the hallway and shone my flashlight around. The answer was, of course, nobody. The hallway was deserted.

Susan began to play back her last burst EVP session. Suddenly, she looked up. "Why is that door moving?"

We all turned to look. The door was slowly swinging shut with an audible creak, closing us inside Hank's room.

"Did you hit the door?" Susan asked, looking at me.

"No. Absolutely not." I was standing too far away from the door to have inadvertently caught it with my elbow or some other part of my body, and besides, I would have felt it if I had made contact.

"I didn't think so. I could see you, and you weren't moving."

The door had been standing open for the past few days, and had not moved in the slightest. Nor were we moving around when it began to close. We had stomped around the second floor hallways countless times over the past four days, and not once had the door changed position.

Nonetheless, we had to carry out our due diligence. Returning the door to its normal open position, we began to stomp on the floorboards, then started jumping up and down in an attempt to see whether the vibrations would transmit into the frame and therefore make the door close once more.

It didn't budge.

So we had a combination of disembodied footsteps out in the hallway, and then roughly five minutes later, the door to Hank's room deciding to close all by itself.

Had Connie's decision to put on Hank's shirt provoked a response, or was one of the other second floor entities responsible?

Erik looked around toward the wall on the left hand side. "Somebody just touched my elbow," he said, puzzled.

"Could you have caught it on the filing cabinet?" Jill asked. Erik shook his head.

"No way. I'm standing too far away." And he was, a good four or five feet away from the metal cabinet. There was nothing within touching distance for him to have caught his elbow on, except for the other investigators, and we would have felt it if he had inadvertently nudged one of us.

"I think that something walked up, looked in the door, and decided to start messing with us," Jill said. The sequence of events ran: Footsteps – door – elbow, working their way from outside the room to inside with us. I wondered whether we had an invisible visitor in our midst.

It seemed like a good idea to see whether we could hunt down the source of the disembodied footsteps, so we made our way out into the hallway and then went toward the staircase.

"It's right here," Jill insisted when we reached the top of the staircase.

"Who is?" I asked.

"Our friend from other night. It's standing right over *there*." She gestured toward the opposite doorway, which led in the direction of the Captain's Corner. "Wait – he just disappeared."

I found it interesting that she was referring to the energy as being that of a male; it would rule out the spirit of either Inez or Suzie as the source of it.

Firing up the SLS, Jill advanced along the corridor in the direction of Inez's room. She caught sight of a tall stick figure, standing halfway down the hallway, a little past the entrance to Suzie's room on the left.

Two knocks came from behind us, back at the top of the stairs. We went back to check, but yet again found nobody there. The game of cat and mouse seemed to be going again. As we reached the top of the stairs, a loud knock or pop came from somewhere off to our right, in one of the old residential rooms.

We headed that way in an attempt to try and identify

the source of the noise. A dull thud came from above us at the far end of the hallway – inside the attic, which we knew full well was empty, as Susan and I had checked it out thoroughly.

For the rest of the night, we were like dogs chasing our own tails. Whenever we would hear anything strange or pick up an odd EMF reading, we would dutifully chase after it, only to be left empty-handed and have the sounds start up somewhere else. Malvern Manor turned out to be maddening in that regard. Josh had been right: It really was one big game of cat and mouse.

Finally, with a long road trip home to Colorado and other states laying ahead of us later that day, we decided to call it.

It was a little disappointing to see that Rosie the doll hadn't moved once during our stay. We left her sitting on a chair in the break room, hoping that future investigators would have a little more luck with the creepy little thing.

Once the equipment was packed away and loaded into the car, we did a walk-around to make sure that everything was as it should be, then locked the door. Standing under the car port, which an earlier visitor seemed to have driven into (it leaned precariously on damaged struts) five of us waited patiently while Stephen performed a variation of his typical protection ritual.

As I mentioned at the beginning of this book, I used to be a great deal more skeptical about such things than I am now, blowing off the idea of 'spiritual protection' (I really didn't believe that there was such a thing) and blithely driving home from haunted locations without a care in the world. That all changed when I brought something particularly nasty home with me after investigating a former hospital. It had forced me to eat a little humble pie; as an avowed agnostic, having to call in my friend Stephen, a Catholic priest, in order to conduct a ceremony of blessing in my own home seemed a little awkward. To his credit, Stephen didn't give me a hard time about it, and duly got rid of what he called "a pair of psychic parasites" in less than an hour. Now I participated in protection rituals whenever I visited a haunted property, whether Stephen was with me or not. It just seemed safer that way.

The experience had taught me to respect the beliefs of others, no matter whether they differed from my own or not, and I therefore waited patiently as Stephen did his thing. He placed containers of blessed water outside the front and rear entrances, stating that it should prevent any unpleasant attachments that future visitors might bring from coming into Malvern Manor; it should also stop any potential hitch-hiking entities from latching onto one of us and following us home.

Stephen stood a little bit straighter and cleared his throat.

"To all of the spirits here: You are not welcome to come with us. You are not permitted to attach yourself to us or follow us. You have no permission to connect with us at any distance, once we have left this property."

He instructed the entire team to envision a white light coming down from above us, suffusing every cell in our body, cleansing and purifying us of any negative energy that we might have developed during our time at Malvern Manor.

The entire process lasted less than ten minutes, at which point Stephen assured us that we were as fully spiritually protected as it was possible for us to be. After one last look at the dark old manor house, we climbed into our rental car and hit the road.

I knew beyond all shadow of a doubt that one day, in the not-so-distant future, I would be going back. Malvern Manor and I weren't done with one another yet.

The journey home gave me ample opportunity to

ponder the haunting of Malvern Manor from multiple angles. Before we get to my own opinions about the case, I'd like to share with you the thoughts of several other investigators who have spent time walking its haunted hallways.

Chapter Eighteen
"I'm awake..."

Jonah Jones's interest in the paranormal stretches all the way back to his early childhood, when he regularly saw the apparition of a man climbing to the top of the stairs in his home.

"I really was so young at the time that there should be no way for me to remember it now," he reflects, "but I can see him right now, as clear as day."

As a grown man, Jonah and a friend became fans of the TV show *Ghost Adventures,* tuning in religiously each time a new episode was aired. They finally tired of just watching; they wanted to progress to *doing,* which is how they found themselves getting involved with their first paranormal investigations. What began with conducting simple burst EVP sessions at home with their phones soon graduated to more structured field investigations, visiting an assortment of haunted places.

He first learned about Malvern Manor from YouTube. A video that Josh had uploaded to the site showed a cabinet door seemingly opening itself on command. Jonah was sufficiently impressed to want to visit the place and see for himself what all the fuss was about.

When he checked on the availability of the building with Josh, Jonah was thrilled to see that the night of his birthday was still open. He wasted no time in snapping up the opportunity to spend a night at the Manor.

Jonah found himself eagerly anticipating the event, and when the day of his birthday finally arrived, he and his team were more than ready to hit the ground running. Sarah Stream met him on his arrival and gave him a walk-through tour of the place. When they went into the parlor, something distinctly unusual happened: Jonah and a fellow team-member heard the sound of a little girl laughing.

When they reached Hank's room, Jonah sensed the presence of what he believed to be the former occupant himself.

"I just felt him on my back," Jonah said. "Literally on my back and breathing down my neck. He didn't want me in his room. My girlfriend, Kylie, felt it too...this overwhelming sensation that we were not welcome."

Considering Hank's distinctly anti-social reputation, that certainly makes sense.

Things took a turn for the bizarre when the small

group reached Gracie's room. Sarah had just finished telling them that Gracie sometimes liked to mess with male visitors, when both Jonah and his fellow investigator, Matt, got their butts pinched.

"It hurt," laughs Jonah, "She pinched it pretty hard."

He went on to say that the entire night was "a giant game of cat and mouse." That made my ears perk up. There was that phrase again, the one that Jonah had used repeatedly: Cat and mouse.

In the Shadow Man's hallway, Kylie went into the bathroom on the left side. When Josh found her, she was crying; she wasn't able to say what was causing it, but Kylie had been overwhelmed by a feeling of great sadness and depression upon entering the room, and it had caught her emotionally off-guard.

"Apart from going to Malvern Manor itself, my biggest birthday wish was to have a spirit say 'Happy birthday' to me. I was standing on the staircase, running a spirit box, and that's exactly what happened. It was absolutely crystal clear. Totally blew me away and made my night."

It was obvious to me during our interview that this was the single event that most stood out in Jonah's mind concerning his first trip to Malvern, but as we spoke, it turned out that there were other experiences which also cannot easily be explained. One such event took place in the nursing home wing. The investigators were shining a strobe light down the hallway, hoping to provoke a little activity of some sort, when everybody present heard the sound of what Jonah describes as "the craziest, disembodied female laugh you ever heard in your entire life!"

"Could that have been the lady who haunts Room 7?" I asked.

"Maybe. She took a dislike to me. I brought her some flowers, trying to be nice, and ended up getting growled at for my trouble! My friend Johnny and I felt really unwelcome in that room, but Kylie felt extremely relaxed and peaceful in there. I guess the lady just really dislikes guys."

"I was really, really drawn to that specific room," Kylie told me. "The story was that the woman who lived in that room had an abusive husband *[this is a slightly different version that the one I was told – RE]* and tore all of her hair out. Johnny and I went into the room, and he felt physically sick; he was actually dry-heaving in the bathroom, the sensation was so overwhelming. He had to leave the room immediately. But I got the feeling that while she wanted him to get out, she wanted me to stay and hang out with her."

"Because you're a woman?"

"Exactly. I think that she has a very deep hatred for men. We did a recording session in there. Every time I mentioned her husband, we would get growls showing up as EVPs on the audio recording."

"We also heard disembodied growls with our own ears," Jonah interjected.

It is interesting to note that only Johnny and Jonah heard the growls with their own ears; Kylie didn't, despite sitting right there in the same room with them...it was almost as if the growls were not intended for her ears, but only for those of the two men.

"Now Hank's room was the exact opposite," Kylie went on. "Whoever was in there really did not like me at all. I was going to try on his clothes in order to try and generate some activity, but when we did the first walk-through, I felt so unwelcome in there that I didn't even want to go near them."

Again, this is completely consistent with the stories concerning Hank's behavior, and his strong dislike for female company – especially when that company goes near his clothing.

When I asked them which part of Malvern Manor had been the most paranormally active for them, they indicated that it was the hallway leading to Suzie's and Inez's rooms. "It's a playful hallway," Jonah said, in response to my question about the dark energy force that we had encountered there, "So we found the energy up there to be very happy and positive...but then it would change, just like that. The whole atmosphere would change, and then there would be this immediate, heavy darkness that would just come down on the place in virtually no time at all.

Jonah had been exploring the second floor, and was walking back past the Captain's Corner when he saw something that stopped him dead in his tracks; a completely black shadow figure walked in front of one of the windows.

"It completely took my breath away," he recalled. "It caught me mid-sentence and I just couldn't finish talking; all I could do was stare at this thing. The shadow figure was completely blocking the street light coming in from that window, and I swear that it was looking right at me."

"You could see its eyes?" I asked.

"No, but I tell you, I could feel it staring at me. It went off in the opposite direction, toward the staircase."

Kylie went on to talk about an experience that she and Johnny had had in Suzie's room. They were using the now-traditional method of getting interaction in that room by coloring in some of the books that had been left on the bed. Suddenly, they were distracted by the sound of a childlike giggling coming from somewhere toward the end of the hallway, in the direction of Inez's room.

"We thought that Inez was messing with us," Kylie recalled, "but since I found out that Inez didn't actually die at Malvern Manor, I'm not sure *what* was laughing at us. When we asked the spirit box who was there with us, we got an intelligent response: the name *Eddie*..."

It was at that point that a second voice, totally distinct from the first, broke through on the spirit box and asked who Eddie was. A second male voice came through the speaker and echoed her question: "Who's Eddie?" The first voice responded with a chilling, *Eddie's dead...*

A couple of minutes later, still another voice came through the spirit box and declared, *There's Eddie*. It was almost as if a newcomer had entered the room and spotted somebody that they recognized.

Only later would Kylie discover that one of the pigeon holes over in the nursing home wing bore the name

Eddie...

When they relocated to the room next door to Suzie's, Jonah clearly heard the sound of footsteps walking around in the corridor directly outside, in the region of the Captain's Corner. Naturally, when Jonah went to check, nobody was there.

"I think that the Shadow Man is actually Eddie," Jonah explained. "I believe that he is the one who is the darkness at Malvern Manor."

"So just to be clear," I said, "Are you saying that this is the spirit of a deceased person, in your opinion?"

"I am, and I think he was a nasty man who now has some real power available to him. We really got messed around with that night. He gave us the real run-around, that cat-and-mouse game Josh likes to talk about. Some people think that the Shadow Man is stuck in that one hallway, but I don't believe that he is; I think that he can roam around the whole building at will, and that he likes to run around Malvern Manor, toying with people."

"For what purpose?"

"Because he enjoys it. I think he really loves to torment people, not just the living, but also the good spirits who are resident there."

It should be pointed out, in the interests of fairness, that even if Jonah's theory is correct and the Shadow Man really is named Eddie, it does not necessarily mean that Eddie was ever a former resident, patient, or employee of Malvern Manor; he could just as easily be a tag-along entity, someone that came along with a visitor to the manor and simply stayed behind when that person left.

"I think that Eddie may be the reason that Suzie is afraid to come out of her room," Kylie interjected. "Everything was nice and friendly in Suzie's room at first, when we were sitting and coloring with her. But as soon as that name, Eddie, came through the spirit box, boom – things changed just like that. It was like Suzie fled as soon as Eddie turned up. It may be that she's scared of him."

One of the tools that Jonah and I both employ is the Boo Buddy, a combination EMF/temperature/vibration sensor, all wrapped up in the body of a teddy bear. Jonah decided that Inez's room was the optimal location to place the ghost hunting bear. In the hallway immediately outside, one of their fellow investigators said that he suddenly felt very cold. At exactly the same moment, Boo Buddy chimed in that it was also feeling cold – an interesting piece of potentially validating supportive evidence, if ever there was one. Of course, it must be pointed out that even a broken clock will tell the correct time twice every day...

Jonah and his team crashed out to catch some shut-eye at around three o'clock in the morning. Before bedding down for a few hours, he made a point of setting up a motion sensor in the area of the Captain's Corner, facing down the hallway in the direction of Inez's room. The sensor was accompanied by a DVR camera and a digital voice recorder.

Because it was extremely cold everywhere else in the Manor, they elected to sleep in the break room, which at least had the electric heaters running to combat the frigid temperature.

The investigators began to prepare their bedding. Just as everybody was getting ready to say goodnight, the motion sensor began to screech.

Something was moving around upstairs.

As any good paranormal investigator would have done, the team went upstairs to check it out. Finding nobody, and getting heartily sick of the cat and mouse routine, they went back downstairs and went to sleep.

The team slept soundly, with no further disturbances...at least, until they reviewed the evidence from their equipment later on.

Approximately ninety minutes after they had returned to the break room and fallen asleep, all hell broke loose upstairs on the second floor. Both the DVR audio track and the digital voice recorder both picked up the same thing: the sound of constant activity, in the form of running and stomping footsteps, moving furniture, and banging and clattering. This cacophony went on for two and a half hours while the astonished investigators could hardly believe their ears.

Perhaps the most remarkable thing of all was that, in the midst of all the clamor that was going on up there on the second floor, Jonah caught a single EVP. It was clearly the sound of a little girl's voice, speaking just two words:

I'm awake...

Chapter Nineteen
Scratched

"I have a little bit of a paranormal hangover," Sarah Stream said at the onset of our interview, "but I guess that's only to be expected."

As a paranormal investigator, Sarah has spent many hours inside Malvern Manor. She feels drawn to the place, and is extremely protective of the building, its spirits, and its reputation. She has logged more hours inside the haunted building than many other investigators.

Sarah had just spent the night probing the secrets of the attic.

"I had a lot of paranormal experiences growing up," she told me when I asked about her background, "and the first time I went out on a real investigation (to the Villisca Ax Murder House) I had a fantastic time. I soon became addicted, and here I am today, still looking for ghosts."

"How did you first get involved with Malvern Manor?" I asked.

"I was attending an event with Dustin Pari. It was one night at Villisca and one night at Malvern. I live nine miles away, and I'm really good friends with Josh, so if I get off work early or have a weekend when my kids aren't home, I just like to hang out at the Manor."

"It sounds almost as though you have a personal attachment to the place."

"Oh, yeah," she affirmed. "And I don't know why that is for sure, but I feel that whatever is up in the attic keeps pulling me back there. Every time I'm there, I have to go up to that attic.

"Whenever I'm up there, there's always a little girl that comes through. I often get EVPs of her."

That led us onto the topic of Inez. What did Sarah think about the ghostly little girl – was it truly the spirit of Inez, or something else entirely?

"I don't think it's really her. I think it's a different girl. I've never gotten a name in the attic, and I don't ever get anything in Inez's room; in fact, I don't even feel the need to be there. Usually I tend not to go down the Captain's hallway at all, unless there are other visitors present who want me to go with them."

Her answer puzzled me a little. "But that's one of the more active areas of the Manor..."

"Yeah, it is," Sarah agreed. "For me, though, I don't

feel a connection in that area, which I do in the attic."

"Have you had any experiences with the male entity that is supposed to haunt the attic – the man who seems to like cigarettes and whisky?"

It turned out that Sarah had. Unlike many visitors, she doesn't usually feel threatened when she is all alone in the attic, and admits to having a fondness for hanging out with grouchy old men (which would make Hank's room a must!)

"I always feel like I'm being watched up there – not necessarily by anything bad, but it *is* constant. When the little girl is present, she will often say things like, *He is here, I'm worried about you,* or *You need to leave...*those kinds of things. Then she'll leave, or at least quit talking, and her voice will be replaced by this growly male voice coming through the spirit box. He shuts her down."

"Have you ever seen him?"

"No, but I *have* seen a lot of shadows up there, usually moving in the corners...but no definite figures or faces."

When I told her that my colleagues and I had experienced no paranormal activity whatsoever up in the attic, Sarah responded that the attic was completely unpredictable in that way; it was just as likely to be absolutely hopping at two o'clock in the afternoon as it was to be utterly quiet by ten o'clock at night.

Sarah believes that whatever it is that dominates the attic also controls the rest of the Manor. She thinks that this same force (the male entity) is responsible for keeping Suzie from leaving her room. Her theory is that one single entity is responsible for much of the paranormal activity throughout the building, and acts as a sort of puppet-master; one single entity with many different facets or presentations.

"A lot of the activity depends on who's up there in the attic," she explained. "Whenever Josh is up there with me, it becomes very apparent that it doesn't like him at all. I have this Canadian friend who happens to be a psychic, and she watches the live feed whenever I'm here. She has described seeing a creepy old man in the crawlspace of the attic, and said that he looked a lot like the character of Mr. Burns from *The Simpsons;* old, extremely frail, wearing baggy clothes, and with a long, beaky nose. He just stands in that little hole up there and watches us.

"She has also seen the little girl, and another male spirit who appears to be mentally disabled. There's also an older lady who puts in an appearance from time to time. But that one guy runs the show, and he won't let the others leave..."

"How was your night last night?" I asked.

"We got a lot of activity in the Shadow Man's hallway. A female voice came through the spirit box and kept repeating the words, *Rape* and *He raped me.* Every time the female voice said that, a deep, growling male voice would follow up with, *No! Be quiet!* It happened ten times in just fifteen minutes.

"Most of my experiences in that hallway have happened in Room 7. The very first night I was there, I remember that a group of people were gathered outside Room 2, being very loud. I don't much like crowds, so I went to Room 7 at the opposite end of the hall to do some solo investigation.

"I sat down, and suddenly the lady who haunts that room grabbed my leg. I've noticed that whenever I'm in that room, even in a small group, if there are any males present, she really doesn't like to talk to them."

This corroborated the story that Jonah and Kylie had told me about their own experiences in Room 7, which had been as different to one another as night and day.

"She definitely doesn't like guys, but if I sit there by

myself I get a lot of activity, a lot of movement, my meters start going crazy...but as soon as a guy walks in the room, it's done.

"I left my recorder running in Room 7 once when it was completely empty. When I played back the audio file, it had picked up the sound of pool balls bouncing off one another."

"There's a pool table in the room just across the hallway," I pointed out.

"Yes, but there aren't any pool balls..."

I asked Sarah her opinion about the entity which Jonah believed was behind the entire haunting, the man named Eddie. She had never heard that name at the Manor before, nor had it turned up on any EVPs. Could this be the same force that Sarah was convinced ruled over Malvern Manor from high up in the attic?"

"Whatever it is, it likes to put on a show," she said. "Eddie may just be one name it goes by, when it suits its purpose. The same could be true for Inez. Whatever's there is trying to make us think that it's all these different things, when in reality I think that it's just a few...or maybe even just one.

"When I was walking past Gracie's room one night, I

swear to you that I saw heard somebody in that room. I heard rustling and breathing. When I poked my head inside and checked with my flashlight, there was nobody in there. One of my fellow investigators was touched in there. I left a Parascope sensing device on the wheelchair next to Gracie's glasses, then went out of the room. When I came back, those glasses were laying on the floor."

This was eerily similar to what had happened to Stephen, when his digital voice recorder had somehow transported itself from a spot on the shelf into his bag, several feet away.

Our interview finally came full circle, ending up at the attic where it had first started. I told Sarah about the attic door opening by itself, and asked whether she had experienced anything similar during her time there.

"It opens itself all the time," she said, telling me that she and Josh regularly closed the door firmly and latching it shut, only for them to go back up an hour later to find it standing wide open once again. "That actually happened yesterday. When I went upstairs, the light in Hank's room had switched itself on – this was after Josh had done his end-of-day walk-through and turned the lights off – and the attic door was standing wide open. The attic light was on. I checked with Josh, and he had definitely turned all those lights off..."

All of which led to the big question: Just why was Malvern Manor haunted in the first place?

"It could be the colorful history of the building," Sarah began, "but I'd like to know what was on that land before it was built. The answer might be found there. It's hard to know for certain."

I asked Sarah what she considered to be one of her most memorable experiences, and she related what had happened the night before. She had gotten a very strong feeling that she should go up to the attic. Taking Josh and several others along, Sarah and her small group started running a spirit box. Her own name came through it a couple of times.

One of the visitors stood up from a crouch, and as he did so, something unseen knocked his hat off in full view of everybody. Sarah was sitting with her back against one of the walls when she suddenly felt a sensation akin to pinpricks across the skin of her back, as though somebody was poking her repeatedly with a tiny needle. She felt herself growing increasingly "spaced out," and finally decided to head downstairs. As she reached the corridor at the bottom,

Sarah stumbled – not tripping mechanically, but more a feeling of being weak and uncoordinated – and had to catch herself.

"Are you alright?" Josh asked, following along behind her.

"I really don't feel right," she admitted. "I feel dizzy, almost...drunk."

"We're getting you outside." Brooking no argument, Josh escorted her to the main staircase. As they reached the top of the stairs, Sarah felt so weak that she was forced to hand her equipment over to Josh so that she could use both handrails in order to prevent herself from falling.

Sarah took the stairs slowly, one at a time, wary of collapsing on the way down. At the midway point, she was suddenly overcome with a sense of great sadness and depression, all for no apparent reason that she could fathom. She fought back the need to burst into tears.

Taking in a little fresh air outside, Sarah slowly composed herself. When she felt better, she asked Josh to examine her back, which they were surprised to see had developed an angry red scratch.

Roughly thirty minutes later, the very same thing happened to another female investigator up in the attic; she also got scratched, though her injury was deeper and more pronounced than Sarah's had been. When the two scratch victims compared notes, they realized that they had both experienced exactly the same symptoms: a sudden onset of dizziness and weakness, and a sense of overwhelming grief at the halfway point on the staircase, followed by a significant scratch on the back.

This second lady, whose name was Amanda, also reported feeling an indefinable attraction toward the attic, being drawn there by some invisible pull. I decided that I'd quite like to talk to Amanda to hear her story for myself. Fortunately, I was able to arrange a phone interview with her.

"My first visit was a public tour with a number of other people," Amanda Borrego began. "At first we thought it was all just hype, but then we went home and realized that we'd caught some growls, a disembodied laugh, and some unexplained mumbling after our first visit, and that convinced us that Malvern Manor was the real deal."

She made arrangements to go back with her team,

Ethereal Paranormal Investigations. During their visit, they conducted a spirit box session in Hank's room. The name 'Hank' came through the box several times in succession. "Hank used a lot of foul language, the sort of words that would not be allowed on air," she laughed, adding that Hank had even gone so far as to call her husband a dick-head!

The night before our interview, Amanda and her team had been back at Malvern Manor and had made contact with a voice calling itself 'Ernie' in that same room. Five investigators were present at the time, but when Amanda asked how many people were actually in the room, she was given the answer, *Eight*...Even when she asked four of five times, the answer remained the same.

Even more surprising was the next interaction, in which the spirit box claimed that Inez was also with them in the room.

I asked Amanda about the attic, which she had spent some time in the night before, accompanied by Sarah Stream. "I felt very discombobulated up there, that feeling you get when you've been drinking, you know? In fact, it was so bad that I had to leave my whole team up there. As soon as I got downstairs, I was overcome with a flood of emotion that I still can't explain. I just leaned against the wall and cried."

It struck me how similar this was to Sarah's own experience.

"When I had calmed down a little, I realized that my back felt like it was on fire," Amanda continued. "I asked my grandma to take a look. She raised up my shirt, and saw that there was a big scratch running down the length of my back." That was exactly what had happened to Sarah.

Even more interesting, as Josh Heard would go on to point out, I had already made arrangements with both Sarah and Amanda to interview them for this book; how odd that of the many people to spend time up in the attic that night, the two interviewees were the only ones to experience this same dizziness, emotional overload, and unexplained marks appearing on their body. Coincidence, or something a little more concerning...?

Chapter Twenty
Johnny Houser

Johnny Houser is a great reason for not judging a book by its cover. Big, bearded, and tattooed, the heavily-muscled custodian of the Villisca Ax Murder House looks as though he could break you in half for looking at him the wrong way. Yet once you get talking to him, it soon becomes apparent that the star of *Johnny Houser Vs...* is one of the nicest, friendliest people you could ever hope to meet.

A few days after kindly taking the time to help us stir up some paranormal activity in the nursing home wing, Johnny graciously consented to an interview regarding his own personal experiences at Malvern Manor.

"I heard stories about this about this new haunted place that were going around," Johnny began, "and so I was able to get in there when the place first opened up. I went over there and met Josh (I knew him already) and so I wanted to give it a try. With a lot of locations, it's a case of 'Go there, spend the night, call it good,' but with Malvern Manor, there's just something that keeps pulling me back."

Based on the episode of *Paranormal Lockdown* in

which Johnny's name can be heard coming through as a possible EVP, it would seem that something at the Manor takes a rather active interest in him. I pointed out that our own equipment had gotten his name several times, he laughed with what I thought was a slightly nervous undertone to his voice. "That's cool but also slightly unsettling at the same time. It's like, 'Why are you talking about me?'"

"You've been there a few times," I said, "but not nearly as many as Josh, who practically lives there."

"I always felt that I was drawn to the Villisca Ax Murder House, and now I think that maybe me coming to the Ax House wasn't the entire picture; maybe I was supposed to go to Malvern, because maybe this is all connected somehow. I'd love to figure out how these two locations are connected – we'd all love to know, wouldn't we? – but good luck with figuring that out! I doubt we'll ever truly know who committed those murders. But I've started to wonder if this is a continuing chapter of something larger."

"If there is a link between those two locations, you yourself are certainly a link too, Johnny. You go back and forth between them both. It also blew us away that you were answering our questions while sitting in the Villisca Ax

Murder House and could hear a thumping coming from somewhere up above your head, in what should have been a totally empty house. Has that ever happened to you before?"

"No, especially not while I'm talking about something so specific – we were talking about Malvern and Villisca when it happened. And you want to know something really strange...?"

"Go ahead," I said, leaning forward attentively.

"After I had talked to you, I was shooting an episode of my show at Villisca. The voice of that little girl – Inez – kept coming through my spirit box, right there inside the Ax Murder House. She spoke four times."

"Do you think that's *really* the spirit of Inez?" I asked. "Or could it be...well, something else?"

"My gut instinct is that it isn't actually her. Who knows, of course, but that's what my gut says..."

Changing tack, I asked Johnny to tell me, in his own words, the story of his encounter with the Shadow Man.

"I dropped by one day, and was just walking around, not actually investigating...it was dusk, starting to get dark. When I'm in a place like Malvern, I like to just wander around, not really looking for anything in particular, but getting a feel for the place, taking in the atmosphere.

"All of a sudden, something shot past me. I caught it in my peripheral vision. I turned to look, and could see a mass at the far end of the nursing wing hallway. It was darker than the surrounding darkness. I leaned forward to look at it, then closed my eyes for a second, opened them, looked away, and looked back...and it was still there.

"So I'm thinking to myself, 'What is that?' That's when it just came right at me. I'd never experienced anything like it before. The thing got right up in my face, and it got there so quick – it was like, *boom!* – there was no sensation of anything passing through me or anything like that, though; it was right there one second, gone the next, in the blink of an eye.

"That's when I thought, Yeah, I'm out of here!"
It's hard to blame Johnny for turning tail and hoofing it. As I sit at my writing desk in my well-lit home office, it's all too easy to wonder why an experienced paranormal investigator would flee when confronted with the very thing that we are desperately trying to seek out; but I have also stood in that exact same spot in the nursing home wing, and let me tell you, the atmosphere over there is something else entirely. Even Josh Heard, a man who knows the Manor as well as anybody still alive, turned and ran when he was rushed by

the Shadow Man. Something about the experience seems to invoke the fight-or-flight reflex in those who encounter this entity on his home turf, no matter how big and bad they may be. I am sure that I would have reacted in the same way if I had undergone the same experience, especially if I was all on my own in the darkness of that haunted hallway. After all, what sane person wouldn't?

Chapter Twenty-One
Dustin Pari

Although Dustin Pari is perhaps best-known for his appearances on the *Ghost Hunters* family of TV shows, he is also a Christian lecturer, motivational speaker, and medical professional. His favored term is 'spiritual researcher.' No stranger to Malvern Manor, he kindly took some time out of his busy schedule to share accounts of his experiences there.

"Malvern Manor is a little bit different from all of the other places I've investigated," he began. "Some of the stories are a little bit darker than the norm, and some of them are very sad...but the Manor left me with a very pleasant feeling, unlike the Villisca Ax Murder House, which felt far less positive. Malvern is a small, beautiful little town, with the diner, one little gas station. It's your classic American small town."

"Josh Heard told me that you were one of the first people to report seeing the very small shadow figures that are now getting more and more common," I said. "Could you please tell me a little bit more about that?"

"Shadow figures are what got me into this field in

the first place. It's always been my experience that they're either two-and-a-half to three feet tall, or they're six feet tall. I don't know if they're actually a human spirit, or what they are exactly; I think that because some of them are shorter, we tend to think of them as being children, especially as the Manor has a history of ghost children being associated with it. We definitely did encounter a short shadow figure while we were there.

"We also had a really great communication session in Inez's room and in the hallway outside, mostly using the Portal device. Something new I decided to try during this last visit – at least, I haven't done it since I was on *Ghost Hunters International* – was to ask questions in Spanish. I'm by no means fluent, but I know enough to ask a few questions and make sense of the answers. I'm a believer in the Theory of Universal Consciousness, and it's my belief that once you pass over, you're no longer restricted to the knowledge and linguistic skills that you possess while you are alive. That may be why we got responses in other languages at Malvern Manor, including Spanish."

I asked Dustin whether he thought that he was truly communicating with the spirit of Inez, given the fact that she had not actually died there. We discussed the possibility that the entity which many believed to be Inez could possibly be some other kind of spirit, either a thought-form or something else masquerading as Inez.

"I personally do not believe that any spirit is ever trapped anywhere," Dustin began, after thinking for a moment. "I strongly doubt that a loving deity would ever lock the doors to the afterlife to anyone, but I do think that some spirits do tend to linger, and don't move on as quickly as others. Some spirits drop by to visit places that were once very familiar, checking in to see what's going on.

"It's possible that Inez has been drawn to the Manor because she lived and died nearby, and hears her name being spoken all the time."

"I have always suspected that spirits don't perceive time in the same way that we do," I replied.

"Absolutely! Time to them is much different. When my buddy Barry Fitzgerald and I were working on *Ghost Hunters International*, we began playing around with the ways in which we tried to capture evidence of spirits. For example, we used a high speed flash and long exposure times. We noticed something very interesting with those long exposures: When we shot images of ourselves, each of us had a long trail behind us while we moved, which is very common. But when we caught a spirit on camera, we would only catch a single sold figure on just one frame. It suggests that they are moving a lot faster than we can possibly catch them."

I found this to be a particularly interesting observation because it reminded me of the Shadow Man, most specifically the way in which he was said to cover half the length of the nursing home wing hallway in the blink of an eye – no living human being could possibly move that fast.

"I didn't encounter the Shadow Man or get charged by him, but I have witnessed fast-moving spirits before. I'll never forget the time at Ohio State Reformatory, down on the ground floor, when I saw one for just a second and then in a flash it had moved all the way across to the other side. Then there was the time at Leap Castle in Ireland. A beautiful place. I was up in the attic with Barry, and we both saw this figure crouching in the corner. As soon as we turned the ultraviolet light on it, this thing shot across the whole expanse of that back wall so quickly, and went right out the window without breaking the glass. It disturbed all the birds in the trees outside, sending them squawking off into the night air; it was so amazing, man. They move a lot quicker in their time, at least as we perceive it, as we do in ours.

"The same is true of audio evidence," Dustin went on, "When we record what sounds like one little tiny blip of sound, which it's easy to mistake for artifact; when you slow it down, it turns out that there's actually a word or two in there. It all comes down to their time versus our time, and the big differences between the two."

"And they're not bound by the same laws and physical restrictions as we are?" I asked.

"Exactly. For sure."

Our conversation turned to the mystery of rooms 16 and 17, and the possibility that what some had claimed to be a repeated sexual assault was actually something of a consensual and loving nature.

"I very much go where I'm guided on investigations," he began. "I don't have any psychic or mediumistic abilities, but I've been doing this for 26 years now, and I believe that we're all spiritually connected in some way, that we all have some level of ability, whether it's developed or not. When we were in there, I kept getting the vibe that the true story wasn't the one that was often being told. Something about it was incorrect.

"I had the feeling that this was a loving relationship,

so I asked some questions along those lines. When I asked whether the gentleman was being attacked in that room, the reply was that he was not. Then when I asked if the two of them had a relationship, I got the words yes and love. I wondered whether one of the staff members was just against that type of relationship, especially as this took place in a different time than the one we're used to, when any kind of love outside of that between a man and a woman might not be easily accepted.

"All of a sudden, everything lit up. The voices became incredibly clear as they came through my laptop's speakers, using the Phasma Box app, and my friend Lee's recorder was picking up the same thing. Multiple bits of evidence coming through on different pieces of equipment is always incredibly validating."

"Did you have any other experiences there that you would consider to be paranormal?"

"I was investigating upstairs in the hallway, just a little further down past the Captain's Corner. There's a weird little closet-like room that some people think was used as a 'time-out' place. Now, when I investigate, I don't just like to go running into a room; I like to go in, set up some equipment, then step out into the hallway and let the equipment do its work, without me interrupting the environment or the energy. Then I ask questions and see what happens.

"On this particular night, we put some equipment in the Captain's room, then we all stood out in the hallway. I just so happened to have my back toward the opening of the time-out room. As I was asking questions into the Captain's room, I began to get this weird little feeling in my back. I didn't think anything of it at the time, mostly because I knew I was standing with my back to a darkened room and, you know, physically it just feels different.

"This woman in front of me suddenly raised her hand to say something, and I felt something poke me in the back. She said that she had seen a figure standing in that room, just as I reacted to getting poked. I have no idea who or what made that physical contact. The lady began to feel faint, to the point where we had to move her further down the hallway to get her away from there. We let her sit on the floor for a while, just to get her bearings again, until she felt a little better."

Next, I asked Dustin whether he had experienced anything in Gracie's room. Although he had spent some time in there, nothing out of the ordinary had taken place during that time.

"Now we get to the million dollar question, Dustin: What do you think it is about Malvern Manor that makes it so active?"

He paused for a moment, considering his response. He agreed with my contention that the vast majority of things that had happened at the Manor were friendly and positive, despite the sometimes fearsome reputation that it has among members of the paranormal community.

"I don't think the Manor has that tragic history that many haunted locations seem to have. Being somebody who has worked in the news media and also is very active in social media, it seems to me that we – as a collective species and society – are drawn to glorify that which is negative. It says a lot about how we're a little bit broken as a society, because we linger on those dark things, we look for them, and we overlook the good things.

"I think that the building itself was a hub of activity for that sleepy little town. At one time, that little hotel next to the railroad was a popular place to be. When it was a nursing home, it was a place where pretty much everybody in that town who got old, ended up being at one time or another. I would also theorize that it isn't remotely the 'Little

Shop of Horrors' that some people make it out to be.

"Yes, it's quite possible that somebody was mistreated at one time or another, with is a godawful thing and should never happen."

"That happens in quite a few care facilities at some point," I said. "But a few bad apples don't make the whole barrel rotten. The vast majority of people who work in facilities like that are decent, hard-working, and good. They do a very tough job under difficult conditions." As a paramedic and EMT for 16 years, I had seen this first-hand many times over. Those who care for others are the closest thing to angels there are on this Earth...except maybe for dogs, of course.

"Yes, I can tell you as a former EMT myself, it still happens today," Dustin agreed sadly. "With some people, healthcare just burns them out. Others just aren't meant for it. But I'm happy to say that based upon my experiences there, Malvern Manor does not seem to be that kind of horrible place. I think that to his credit, Josh does a great job of showing both sides of the story, and doesn't do what some people do in order to make a 'haunted attraction.' That's why I like going there so much; it's not all gloom and doom. He treats the spirits that linger there – and those who visit – with respect. That's a very important distinction, and one which separates Malvern Manor from a lot of other places."

"He also looks a lot like Kiefer Sutherland," I deadpanned. Dustin burst into laughter.

"That doesn't hurt!"

"I do think that there are some energies there, but I also think that many of them are not. I wrote a book called *The World's Most Haunted Hospitals,* and while I was researching it, I was very much encouraged to discover just how many doctors and nurses seem to still be on duty and caring for patients, long after they had physically died."

"It's who we are as human beings," he agreed. "It's nothing to do with training. It's either in you, or it's not. There's good and bad in the spirit world, just as there is in our world. Just because somebody is negative and angry and cantankerous, that doesn't mean that you're dealing with something demonic. Television does a horrible job of playing that danged 'demon' card all the time. The truth is, sometimes you just get miserable people! Those miserable spirits linger and hang around sometimes for their own reasons."

My mind went directly to Hank, the grouchy old fellow whose crotchety behavior was now an integral part of

Malvern Manor lore. Could he be one such spirit?

"They cause problems just to cause problems," Dustin continued, "and often it's a chance encounter. It's just like going to the store; you could get a cashier that's nice, or you could get somebody that's a jerk."

"And the mood of those people, whether spirit beings or flesh and blood, changes with the circumstances also," I added.

"Right. I think that we tend to attract like-minded individuals to ourselves."

Dustin had given me plenty of food for thought. The more I considered it, the more I came to agree with his point of view. There were good spirits and bad spirits at Malvern Manor, just as there are good people and bad people wandering the streets every day. None of them were entirely good or bad; I strongly suspected that for many of those entities, the manner in which visitors treated them (how provocative or respectful they were) played a key part in the response that they gave in return.

Yet there were still unanswered questions that nagged at me.

Who – or what – was the dark entity that had pursued Jill and Erik down the staircase, the one that we had been warned about? Jonah Jones had his own firm beliefs about the identity of that particular spirit, believing it to be a deceased man named Eddie, but personally I wasn't quite so sure. I respected Jonah's opinion, but I didn't think that there was sufficient evidence to clearly identify that entity. Who knows, Jonah may turn out to be right, but at the time of writing, I think that the jury is still out. It is my belief that the dark spirit is not the ghost of Captain Cullers, who seems to keep a watchful and protective eye over goings-on at Malvern Manor; this entity seems to have less wholesome motives.

Is the being that answers to the name of Inez truly the spirit of that young girl, tragically taken before her time, still haunting the corridors of Malvern Manor today – a place that we have no evidence she ever visited during her lifetime? Or could something else have assumed her name, perhaps a thought-form conjured into existence by the thoughts and beliefs of thousands of visitors, a tangible manifestation of collective mental power that is sufficiently strong enough to run up and down the hallways, laughing, giggling, and speaking to visitors?

Perhaps more ominously, has another spirit chosen to pass itself off as the ghost of Inez, in order to further its own agenda? There are those who work in the paranormal field that like to claim that what may at first appear to be a harmless childlike figure can actually turn out to be something a great deal more sinister. Further research into the identity of this particular spirit is warranted, and I encourage future investigators to Malvern Manor to delve into this particular mystery if they have the time. The truth may turn out to be stranger than fiction.

What of Gracie, the lady with the multiple personalities? Have some traces of those personalities remained behind, long after she herself has gone? Is it possible for multiple fragments of the human essence to remain behind after death? We don't know what ultimately happened to Gracie, and I believe that it would be inappropriate for me to attempt to trace her whereabouts. It may be that she is still alive and living in another long-term care facility, though I think this unlikely. What can be said is that something lingers in her former room. Whether that something can be classed as a haunting, an echo, or something else entirely still remains to be seen.

One of the greatest mysteries of all is that of the Shadow Man. Just who is the shadowy figure that appears outside the doorway of Room 2, then charges toward unsuspecting visitors before disappearing right in front of their eyes? Is this the spirit of the tall man who once resided in that room, said to be the terror of the nursing staff? Without delving into medical records, it is impossible to determine just how much truth there is to the story of this particular patient having a homicidal past. We have only the word of former employees to go on. Yet the Shadow Man has been encountered by several visitors to Malvern Manor, and always seems to act in exactly the same way. Could it be that we are not dealing with an intelligent haunting at all, but rather are looking at a residual apparition, some form of paranormal recording? The possibility is an intriguing one. Josh is keeping a close record of the events taking place in that particular hallway, in the hopes of determining whether there is a pattern to the appearances of the Shadow Man. So far, there appears to be no common thread running through the times at which he has been encountered. Those who experience a Shadow Man sighting are invariably shaken and terrified, often fleeing the nursing home wing in the aftermath of the experience.

Last but by no means least, we come to the Villisca connection. Rumors of there being a link between the ax murders and Malvern Manor have been circulating for quite some time now, and while the results of our glass divination session may not constitute a solid form of proof, I cannot help but wonder whether one day an enterprising and diligent historian will uncover the truth behind that brutal crime...and if, once the perpetrator or perpetrators are finally unmasked, it will turn out that they spent the night at the hotel which would one day become known as Malvern Manor.

The Manor is a place which holds its secrets close. People such as Josh Heard, Sarah Stream, Jonah Jones, and many other paranormal investigators are all working to uncover some of those secrets. Each investigation unearths another piece of the huge jigsaw puzzle which, taken as a whole, can be described as the haunting of Malvern Manor. If you should ever find yourself traveling through the great state of Iowa, then I encourage you, dear reader, to make a detour, preferably for a night but perhaps only for a few hours, in order to step across the threshold and wander those haunted hallways for yourself.

If you do, please let me know what you find. I suspect that the spirits will be only too happy to welcome you.

Chapter Twenty-Two
The Guest-Books

The sheer volume of eyewitness testimony that supports the haunting of Malvern Manor is documented in a series of guest books, in which visitors are invited to record their ghostly experiences for posterity. Unfortunately, a huge chunk of the location's haunted history is now lost, because an unscrupulous visitor stole the original guest book. At the time of writing, its whereabouts are still unknown.

Josh keeps a close eye on the replacement guestbook, which has already been filled and expanded into a second volume. This chapter of the book contains details of some of the more interesting entries. As the stories mount up, the astute reader will notice that a pattern gradually emerges: certain paranormal experiences seem to recur over and over again.

Let's begin with the story of a team that consisted of three female paranormal investigators who reportedly experienced the sound of disembodied footsteps going up and down the empty staircase during their visit. As they were investigating over on the nursing wing, the sound of footsteps once again came toward them from the direction of Room 7, heading toward the nurses' station.

The ever-present equipment failures that seem to plague so many paranormal investigators at Malvern Manor struck once again. While conducting an EVP session in Gracie's room (one in which disembodied voices were heard and an unexplained shadow flitted across the top of the doorway) the batteries died in a walkie-talkie. They were brand new and had been freshly installed beforehand.

The footsteps persisted when the team relocated upstairs to the second floor, and the number of shadow figure sightings increased. One particularly notable shadow figure was spotted when the ladies were conducting an EVP session in the area of hallway frequented by the Captain. The apparition was small, about the size of a young child, and the investigators were convinced that whatever it was, it was by no means benevolent.

When the doors to the individual rooms are closed, shutting out most of the light from the street outside, the second floor is naturally very dark. On this particular night, the team claimed that the light fluctuated, brightening and darkening in a series of 'waves.' While this is not an uncommon thing to occur on paranormal investigations – my team and I have experienced it for ourselves – it is also an extremely subjective one. Unless you have the equipment set up to accurately measure the levels of light at the location you are investigating, it is all too easy for your brain and eyes to play tricks on you, particularly when your surroundings are poorly-lit.

We are on more solid ground when it comes to Electronic Voice Phenomena, which are both recordable and re-playable, and can therefore be analyzed and dissected. The team recorded a number of inexplicable noises and voices, perhaps one of the more interesting being the sound of something being dragged along the floor in Gracie's room. This happened while the room was empty, with the investigators conducting research in other parts of the Manor. Gracie's room definitely seems to be an EVP hot-spot, though exactly what was being dragged remains a mystery.

Over on the nursing home wing, the ladies recorded what sounded like a plastic water bottle popping, followed by the sound of running water. As with the recording from Gracie's room, no source was ever identified.

During the course of my investigation, we got virtually no evidence of paranormal activity in the parlor, aside from a spirit box interaction. One member of this particular group had an experience to remember when she felt her hair being brushed by an unseen force of some kind. After relocating to the attic, the team heard a meowing sound, which presumably came from a cat. It should be pointed out that a friendly domesticated cat does roam the neighborhood, and often turns up at the back door of Malvern Manor with the hope of being fed (several entries in the guest-book mention it). However, even when we take into account the fact that sound travels further at night, it seems rather unlikely that the sound of it *miaowing* would be audible two stories up in a sealed attic. Of course, the only way to debunk this conclusively would be to test the theory with an actual cat.

The ubiquitous power drains bugged this group of investigators too. After setting up their laser grid device with fresh batteries, they found that they had completely drained in under three minutes, a ludicrously short amount of time. Thinking that perhaps the batteries were duds, they replaced them with another set and tried again. The same thing happened. Three minutes' worth of life is almost unheard of for AA batteries. To add insult to injury, the ladies' camera died as well, and flatly refused to function for over an hour.

Perhaps something at the Manor did not want to be seen that night.

It's both surprising and perhaps a little concerning that somebody might bring children to a place like Malvern Manor, but a number of kids have visited over the last few years. Most are simply taking the guided tour with their parents, but one or two have actually spent the night. Sometimes they get more than they bargained for.

One ten-year-old wrote her own entry in the guest book, declaring that she had felt as if her hair was being touched and was burning. The same child claimed that when she was up in the attic, she had felt as if she was being punched in the stomach and had heard the sound of furniture moving around by itself.

Most interesting of all, the girl reported hearing and having recorded the sound of a child singing up in Inez's room during an EVP session. If this is true, could the spirit which claims to be Inez have been attracted to another young girl that was close to her own age when she had died – or did it perhaps have a more sinister motive for singing to her?

Another visitor claimed to have captured the image of a tall man standing outside Room 2 – the same location from which the Shadow Man appeared and rushed Johnny Houser. She also reported "many orbs flying about." Like most paranormal investigators, I take the view that most so-called 'orbs' are no more than flying dust particles, so I tend to dismiss such claims.

Something I *cannot* dismiss is what this particular visitor describes happening in the nursing wing. When I chanced upon this particular page of the guest book, I could hardly believe what I was seeing:

> *2nd time entering the nurses' area, EVP recorder caught a moan at 8:45.*

This visitor recorded a moan in the same part of the building where the six members of my group also heard and recorded a moan. Coincidence? I'm inclined to think not. The question then becomes whether this is an intelligent entity, something that is trying to communicate, attempting to express its fear or anger to those who enter the nursing wing, or whether it is an entirely residual audible phenomenon, something no more sentient than an MP3 file.

The same group experienced a multitude of EVPs during their time at Malvern Manor. For instance, they heard what sounded like an unexplained moaning or yelling noise upstairs in Inez's room. They had deployed voice recorders in multiple rooms all around the Manor. While they were sitting in the break room and trying to get warm, the recorder that had been left running in the attic picked up the sound of a train going by. No big deal, one might think; but the train sounded extremely close to the Manor, and yet none of the investigators down on the ground floor heard a thing. (I can testify to the fact that when a train passes by in the distance, it is easily heard from the break room. It happened to us multiple times.)

Their recorders also picked up the clear sounds of music emanating from different parts of the building, including both the entertainment room and Inez's room, from which unexplained knocks and taps were also recorded. Slightly more disturbing was the sound of a little girl's voice humming along...

The sound of two men having a conversation in the entertainment room turned up on one of the recordings, as were the sounds of something like a piece of furniture being dragged around in the attic; this last piece of audio sounds very much like that reported by the ten-year-old girl. It was followed by the sound of a piano playing(!) and a male voice saying the words, "Oh my God." Although the sound of voices from people walking by outside can definitely carry up to the attic, it is practically impossible to make out anything that is being said. They are simply too muffled.

It seems that this particular group had an extraordinary amount of luck recording EVPs. Another visitor was no less impressed but was a little more succinct about detailing them:

> *Great time! Knocks, screams, shadows, footsteps,*
> *and had things touch us. Shadow ran up on me.*
> *Caught steps on recorder.*

Another instance of a shadow figure rushing up to a visitor. Such aggressive behavior is actually not the norm for shadow figures, in my experience; they tend to adopt more of a lurk/run/hide approach when confronted by inquisitive paranormal investigators. I dearly wish that this visitor had documented the location of their encounter. My money would be on the hallway of the nursing wing...

The next night, a different team was conducting a

spirit box session upstairs in the attic. Although they were prepared for almost anything (such as their own names coming through the device, one after the other) they were taken aback when the sound of rocks and pebbles bouncing off the floor around them suggested that they were under some form of attack. They also recorded the sound a little girl's voice inside the house.

Malvern Manor sat empty for the next few days. The next set of visitors, a man and a woman from Omaha, Nebraska, heard the sound of voices coming from the sole working restroom in the Manor, located on the ground floor next to the break room. As best they could tell, the voices were those of two men and an old lady. This was at around 5:30 in the afternoon. An hour later, while they were taking photographs up on the second floor, they captured the image of a large black male shadow figure standing in the vicinity of the Captain's Corner.

> *Scary as hell!* their journal entry says. *Glad we didn't look @ pictures until later in the evening. Was hard to go back upstairs.*

They also claimed to have recorded "many EVPs," most of which were asking for some kind of help. A voice recorder left running in Gracie's room picked up the sound of a voice saying, "Please help us now." The clearest of the bunch said, "We want you to go back to attic," followed by, "We want you to watch."

In addition to capturing such a diverse array of voice phenomena, these visitors also reported hearing a series of unexplained taps and knocks in the kitchen. Generally, my first instinct would be to point out that a kitchen is usually one of the noisier rooms in any building; refrigerators, ovens, pipes and other gadgets can all team up to generate a host of noises. Malvern Manor's kitchen is rarely used to prepare food, however, and my team and I didn't experience anything remotely like this during our stay. Assuming that the visitors ruled out the more mundane causes such as the air conditioning system, the source of that knocking and tapping remains a mystery.

My team has a strict "zero tolerance" policy when it comes to conducting a paranormal investigation, on the premise that even one drink can impair judgment and the senses to a greater or lesser degree, depending on the individual. Not everybody likes to see it that way, however, such as the three-person team that left this story in the visitor's book:

> *11:00 Went to gas station to get beer. Left a*
> *recording, heard a lot of screeches and a voice*
> *either say "Your [sic] afraid" or "I'm afraid." Not*
> *too sure...*

Slightly more reliable is the entry from a Missouri-based
group [Paranomalies Investigative Team] who found their
initial tour with Josh to be a little frustrating because their
digital voice recorder stopped recording no less than
eighteen times. While standing in the stairwell, they
distinctly heard a voice say the word, "Wow."

     Up in the attic, where the frightening apparition of a
disheveled man has been seen, an investigator was surprised
to find the voice of a man crooning the word
"helllllllooooooo" into her ear. After climbing back down
into the second floor hallway, two investigators were
physically touched by something unseen. The first felt her
hair being gently played with; perhaps more concerning, the
second investigator happened to be bending down and
picking up an item of equipment when she felt a hand
running along the length of her back.

     Over in that old favorite, the nursing wing, a male
investigator must have been quite startled when a block of

wood came flying out of the darkness and hit him on the hand, sending the digital voice recorder he was holding crashing to the ground.

A week later, another visiting team recorded a faint whistling noise in Inez's room, accompanied by the faint voice of a little girl. After switching locations to Suzie's room, they witnessed one of her crayons rolling across the top of the cabinet. Two of their investigators heard the sound of footsteps following them as they made their way to the bathroom. The team left a cell phone recording in the empty attic; upon playback, the sound of people talking and walking around could be heard on the recording.

The team relocated once again, this time to Henry's room up on the second floor. They were talking about Malvern Manor's history when they were interrupted by the sound of heavy footsteps thudding up the main staircase; naturally, when somebody went to check, there was nobody to be found.

Deciding to move back downstairs, they went into the parlor. During an EVP session, the investigators witnessed one of the wheelchairs move all by itself. No doubt impressed, the team decided to try their luck in Gracie's room. One of the male investigators sat in Gracie's wheelchair, and got the repeated impression that somebody was grabbing at him. He soon became light-headed, and believed that something was leeching away his energy.

I found the guestbook to be very useful and informative, but one particular entry was laugh out loud funny. Rather than comment on it, I'm just going to reproduce it here in its entirety. It is simply too good not to share:

> *2am*
>
> *Our friend ******** wanted to check out the attic and we were like f*** no. Y'all can go. Its almost 2am and me, ******* and ****** already experienced some creepy shit up there so were [we're] f***ing Gucci on that. Were [we're] a bunch of f****** pussies. I swear to the lord Jesus Christ Im ready to f***ing leave.*
>
> *F***. This. Shit.*

Apparently somebody was less than thrilled with their visit to Malvern Manor...

Normality returned with the next batch of visitors, who said that they had photographed a tall shadow figure standing behind one of their party in the nursing wing. They also obtained two EVPs, one saying *We're closed,* and the other saying, *I'm sorry.*

It's a wise idea to be skeptical of any supposedly haunted location that provides apparently spectacular evidence night after night after night, and so I was happy to read a report written by a team that had experienced relatively little during their overnight stay at Malvern Manor. They received no class A or B EVPs (anything lower than a B can often be written off as auditory pareidolia) and experienced no visual phenomena, and admitted that the spirit box and Ovilus devices they used produced nonsensical results.

If the author of the next entry is to be believed, the Manor was back on form the following week. The new team claimed that they had picked up on the presence of two spirits in the nursing wing, located outside Room 2, and that they saw a pair of "translucent legs" walking toward them from that location. (If so, that deviates from the more commonly-reported behavior of the Shadow Man rushing at visiting investigators).

I swear there is always someone in the kitchen, the visitor continued, *lots of taps and creaks.* This tallies with the opinion of several other visiting investigators.

The next group reported hearing the sound of footsteps in the empty attic and apparently little else; the team that followed them had a more active time of it, with one of their investigators being punched in the arm by an unseen entity. The nursing wing drained many sets of their batteries, and several of their rechargeable cameras also lost power outside what the writer referred to as 'the shadow room,' presumably Room 2.

Another relatively quiet night awaited the team which followed them, although it wasn't without at least a few interesting experiences. During an early morning EVP session up on the second floor, two paranormal investigators were convinced that they were physically touched; there were a number of EMF spikes with no apparent source; and "strange noises in the halls."

In keeping with the claims of a man who craves alcohol haunting the attic, the next team reported getting some strong EMF swings up there, particularly when they made references to obtaining some whisky. One of the few groups to have used a Ouija board at Malvern Manor, they reported making contact with an entity named Robert who claims to be resident in Room 8.

Another all-female team arrived next. They reported hearing the sound of a dog barking from somewhere within the building just as they were climbing the main staircase. After using a Ouija board to try and connect with the spirit of Hank in his room – unsuccessfully, as it turned out; their efforts were rebuffed every time – and investigating elsewhere throughout the Manor, the group of five settled down in the break room to get some sleep. At 4:13 in the morning, one of the investigators suddenly sat bolt upright and boomed, *GO!* before laying back down and going right back to sleep again.

At 8:45 the following morning, the entire house shook to the noise of what sounded like something very big and heavy being dragged across the floor up on the second floor. As best they could tell, these vibrations were originating from somewhere on the north side. The entire team charged upstairs and set about trying to figure out exactly what the cause was; everything seemed to be undisturbed, left exactly as they had first found it on their arrival the night before.

The smell in Gracie's room can be overpowering, wrote the next group of visitors, before adding the following warning: *Don't accidentally insult her. Rooms 17 and 18 very active. Hank's room spirits will carry their own conversation over the SB-7 [spirit box]. Plenty of activity throughout the place. Can't wait to return.*

The overpowering smell that is believed to signify Gracie's presence was echoed by those who came to the Manor next, who said that future visitors should be on their guard for sudden and distinctive odors. They claimed to run into a number of spirits during their stay, most of whom were curious as to what the newcomers were doing there at Malvern Manor; two were said to be "very verbal with women, but backed off when there was a man in the room."

Coming in next was a team of two females, who focused much of their attention on the nursing wing. They set up a paired laser grid and camera, both aimed down the length of the hallway, and picked up what appeared to be a hand – one which didn't belong to either of them, as they were standing a fair distance away from the camera. They followed up with an EVP session during which the entity that they were communicating with obliged them by covering up specific lights on the laser grid when the ladies asked them to do so. At the end of the session, they were surprised to find that the laser grid had switched itself off...something which should not have been possible, as they had physically taped the 'on' switch down.

In addition to this, the ladies witnessed a lot of knocking and rapping throughout the structure, accompanied by a number of cold spots and temperature changes. While this isn't necessarily paranormal (Malvern Manor isn't exactly a well-insulated building these days) cold spots are often an indicator of paranormal activity taking place.

When they employed a Geo Box up in the attic, the sound of a voice speaking in fluent German came through. Hank's voice also came through and warned them in no uncertain terms to stay away from his room. They dutifully ignored this warning and made Hank's room their next port of call. The spirit of Hank refused to play ball. This is very much in keeping with his reputation for taking a disliking to female visitors (another notation in the guest book states that Hank always sent the spirit board's planchette to GOODBYE whenever the participants were women) and what they took to be his voice ultimately came through the Geo Box once more and told them to leave.

Doubling down, the ladies must have recalled that Hank apparently does not like anybody messing with his clothes – particularly women. One of the investigators put on his shirt, and was rewarded with an angry, *put it back!* from the Geo Box. Something then grabbed her by the arm. The Geo Box yelled, *Leave!* Quite understandably, they did just that, replacing his shirt carefully in the drawer and making tracks.

The investigators felt that their time in the attic and in Hank's room severely depleted their energy, so much so that by the time they made their way downstairs, each of them was feeling weak and dizzy. Just as we had, they used a Boo Buddy teddy bear sensor, leaving it running downstairs. The device kept alarming consistently between 2am and 4am, suggesting that something may have found it interesting enough to try and play with it.

In an eerie parallel with what had happened to a former group, the investigators were both sitting in the hallway of the nursing home wing, when suddenly they heard the sound of a colossal *bang* emanate from somewhere upstairs. Whatever caused the impact was so hefty that it made the building shake. It may or may not be significant that both of the teams that reported this were comprised entirely of female investigators. Something else that the two teams had in common was that they had both gone into Hank's room during the course of their investigation and had apparently managed to get on his bad side. Was someone – possibly Hank, possibly something else – expressing their distaste for the presence of women? If so, assuming that its intention was to scare them off, the mysterious entity was unsuccessful – the two ladies wrote that they "had a blast!"

A few days later, a larger group of six people began their investigation in Hank's room. Exactly as my own team and I had experienced, the door closed itself on them while they were standing in there. Later on, two of their number reported seeing the Shadow Man standing outside the door of Room 2 – this time, he was apparently not in the mood to rush anybody. At the opposite end of the nursing wing hallway, they also claimed to have captured the image of an old woman standing in the doorway of Room 7; she is described as wearing brown pants and a white top. The team also say that later on, they photographed a black mist of some sort in that same spot. It is difficult to comment without actually seeing the photographs.

The team heard a loud crash emanating from one of the hallways while they were standing at the nurses' station – no cause was identified. One of them believed that she saw a white mist in the doorway of Inez's room. Lastly, the kitchen doorknob turned itself several times, despite nobody physically being there when the investigators checked.

The next bunch of visitors was even larger, some nine people in all. At a little after eight o'clock in the evening, as the group congregated in the kitchen and were planning the night's investigation, one of their number wandered out into the break room. When he returned, he claimed to have heard the sound of a little girl's voice coming from somewhere upstairs. Taking another investigator along with him, he went to the bottom of the stairs and called out a greeting. While he probably wasn't really expecting a reply, one can only imagine what it felt like when what sounded like a child answered back from somewhere up above them with a definite, *Hello.* When the intrepid duo went to check the second floor, there was not a soul to be found.

Having heard the story of Gracie, the group decided to conduct an EVP session in what was once her room.

Although it would be a tight squeeze cramming nine people in there, apparently they managed to do so. As discussion turned to the subject of the Multiple Personality Disorder with which Gracie had been afflicted, one of the investigators made a remark about just how difficult it must be to live with such a condition. Although nothing odd was heard at the time, on playing back the recording a soft voice was heard to say, *Uh-huh,* as though in complete agreement. When leaving Gracie's room, one of the team caught sight of what looked like an arm emerging from one of the doorways in the same corridor. It was gone before they could take a picture.

The team decamped to Hank's room next, where they recorded multiple instances of an unexplained whistling. One of their EMF detectors registered massive spikes of energy at intermittent intervals, while a second unit situated right next to it registered none of them. It must be asked when each of these devices was last calibrated, as a non-paranormal explanation should always be the first approach to pursue, but considering just how active Hank's room has been known to be, I certainly wouldn't rule out a paranormal one either.

Their last stop was Inez's room, where they

experienced more apparently random EMF spikes and whistling. Footsteps were heard in the empty hallway outside, where the Captain is believed to prowl.

Next was a return visit from the two female investigators that had so annoyed Hank, and this time they were bringing friends along with them. This time, they were staying for several days and nights. Things appear to have kicked off as soon as the team got started at five o'clock in the afternoon, when one of the investigators caught sight of a shadow figure walking along the corridor that leads to the office. The sound of footsteps was also heard.

In an attempt to stimulate some paranormal activity, the ladies played music from the 1950s in the parlor. They say that this caused them to feel a strong upswell of energy and started to wake the Manor up. Their next stop was the nursing wing, where they claim to have encountered a shadow figure named Johnny and another shadowy entity in one of the old patient rooms that shoved one of the investigators, propelling her some three feet through the air.

When my team and I used a spirit box at Malvern Manor, I think it's fair to say that we had mixed results. By far the most impressive 'hit' as far as I am concerned was when a voice coming through the box correctly identified the fact that we had eaten barbecue the night before. What happened to this particular group of visitors sounds entirely more sinister. According to their written account in the guest book, their Geo Box continually repeated the terms *Son of Satan, Basement, Blood,* and *Kill,* then set about trying to convince them to go down into the basement themselves.

Access to the basement is possible with the permission of the owners. It is little more than a collection of pipes, electrical wiring, and wooden shoring. I didn't spend much time down there personally because it was apparent that anything approaching actual investigation would be pointless; there were simply too many environmental contaminants to contend with. This particular team decided to venture down there themselves, with rather alarming consequences – a blessed crystal that was being worn as a necklace by one of the ladies was yanked from her neck and tossed aside. Assuming that this is exactly what happened, we can infer a malevolent intent on the part of whatever force or entity ripped away the necklace, as such stones are often used as spiritual protection. A male investigator emerged from the basement with a hand-print on one of his arms, along with several scratches. The message seems to be very plain: whatever was down there most definitely did not want company. Could it possibly have been the malevolent entity that we had been warned about when we first arrived at Malvern Manor?

The following morning, one of the female investigators was rudely awoken by the sound of a young girl running up and down the corridors, giggling and laughing. They believe that this was Inez, and attempted to engage with her by reading her a story. According to the entry in the guest book, they were rewarded for their trouble with an EVP.

I am not sure how this team gleaned the information that is listed next, but I have chosen to reproduce it verbatim here as it tracks with what we have been told about the mysterious entity known as "Number One:"

> *"#1" was/is a very evil spirit or possibly demonic. He came to Malvern with the doll [Rosie] and has no respect, much less care, for any other spirit in the Manor. Lots of troubles getting anyone to speak over the Geobox tonight. #1 seemed to be blocking everyone from speaking.*

Josh confirms that Number One is highly disruptive, and

seems to act as though he/she/it rules the roost. Was Number One responsible for the hand print, scratches, and yanking of the blessed crystal necklace down in the basement? It seems to be a reasonable assumption. It may also have been the same dark force that pursued Jill and Erik along the second floor corridor and down the staircase.

If the team expected things to quieten down the next day, they were to be mistaken. Loud footsteps and unexplained knocks sounded throughout the Manor, and were soon joined by disembodied voices, laughter, and on a more ominous note, screaming. No source was ever identified for any of these bizarre noises. One such scream, which seemed to originate from somewhere up on the second floor, was so loud and piercing that the investigators were forced to cover their ears. The investigators did catch sight of a shadow figure at the end of the hallway by the attic entrance. They described it as being tall and lanky, and while the figure made several appearances throughout the course of the day, it always disappeared before anybody could approach it.

It would appear that at least one of the resident entities does not approve of smoking. When the visitors attempted to go outside for a cigarette break, the door flatly refused to open – despite being unlocked. They were finally able to force the door open and leave.

Later that same day, a different team took up residence. Perhaps the spirits had had their fill up playing cat and mouse with the living, because this new batch of visitors experienced nothing paranormal at all. Although there was some initial excitement at the sound of loud bangs coming from the direction of the parlor early the next morning, they were soon able to debunk these as being the sounds of the trash collectors making their rounds.

I have often wondered if the nights on which a very active location suddenly goes flat when a new team arrives can be put down to the different energies that the newcomers bring with them. Can somebody be the equivalent of a psychic "dampener," for example, unwittingly suppressing the levels of psychic energy and preventing paranormal activity from taking place? If so, this would go some way to explaining the wildly divergent results that different groups often experience at the same location. (It must also be pointed out that some people are simply more credulous than others, and are a little too quick to mistakenly attribute a paranormal explanation to every creaking floorboard and clanking pipe).

At any rate, business as normal resumed the following day when a fresh set of visitors turned up. While investigating the nursing wing, they heard the sound of a young girl giggling. Gracie's room, which I say from personal experience usually smells just a little bit musty, was suddenly filled with the stench of stale and rancid urine.

The following night, yet another team received quite the surprise in Inez's room when they claim to have captured something completely unexpected on video: the sight of a torso, which appeared from behind the door and moved across the room to finally disappear inside the closet.

The 4th of July brought extra cause for celebration to the latest residents of Malvern Manor. As so many had before them, they elected to focus much of their time in the nursing home wing, where a particularly intrepid investigator knocked sharply three times on the door of Room 2. The entire team witnessed the sound of three knocks coming right back in response. Unfortunately, Room 2 is securely padlocked as it rented out for personal storage, so it was impossible for the team to go in and verify that the room was truly empty; however, I find the very idea of a keyholder being able to enter the room, hide themselves in there on the off-chance that the visiting investigators would knock on the door, and perhaps most importantly somehow manage to lock the padlock on the door behind them from the inside, to be nothing short of laughable. This is one of those instances in which a paranormal explanation is far less convoluted than a 'normal' one would be.

Not every team gets to experience a sighting of the Shadow Man, but he did put in an appearance on Independence Day. While the Shadow Man didn't seem to be in the mood to charge anybody this time, he did visibly linger at the end of the hallway outside his room, seeming to tease the visiting investigators with his presence.

Up on the second floor, Suzie's bed was squeaking, despite her room being empty. The only thing on top of the bed was the array of coloring books left by visitors and a handful of crayons. A sudden cold spot was reported in the area of the Captain's Corner at around the same time, and the sound of footsteps was heard from the top of the main staircase.

Exhausted, the team decided to bed down in the break room at a little after two o'clock in the morning. They were awoken several times that morning to the sounds of all hell breaking loose upstairs on the second floor; footsteps, laughter, and furniture seemingly being dragged around.

Everybody on the team was accounted for at the time, and nobody was upstairs when all of this was going on. This seems to be a fairly common occurrence at Malvern Manor: when investigators let their guard down and go to sleep, paranormal activity ramps up on the second floor.

Things changed up once again for the next crop of visitors. This time out, the second floor went from being one big paranormal hot-spot to being completely inert throughout the course of their stay. True to form, however, the nursing wing hallway was active, providing the team with a multitude of unexplained noises. Their SLS camera also died without apparent cause, flatly refusing to function after being placed in the nursing home wing.

Malvern Manor stayed active for yet another team, who also experienced disembodied footsteps thudding up and down the long-abandoned hallways. An investigator was poked in the back, and sessions in Inez's room with an Ovilus and a Spirit Box yielded such interesting results as *Child* and *Hang.*

During a session in Gracie's room, a voice came through the Spirit Box instructing them to run. When they asked for clarification – "do you mean that we should run away?" – the same voice responded with a definite, *Yes.* The voice then went on to call each of the investigators present by name. One of the investigators was called by her nickname, which nobody had referred to her by during their time at Malvern Manor, but just so happened to be emblazoned across the back of her shirt.

As the night was drawing to a close, one of the group looked outside and saw that the lights in the nearby church were still switched on. "Maybe we should go over there and get blessed," the investigator remarked.

Yes, you should, a voice from the Spirit Box agreed.

The Manor had no visitors for the next five days. When visitors returned, the place seemed to have recharged its batteries; it certainly gave them a night to remember, at any rate.

"Is this really you, Gracie?" asked one member of the group during an EVP session in her room. "Just say yes."

During the audio file playback, a voice was heard to mutter, *Yeah.* At the same time, a pink plastic ball rolled across the floor under its own steam.

Disembodied moans were heard coming from upstairs. It will come as no surprise to learn that when the team went up to check, the second floor was totally empty, but when they looked into Inez's room, they noticed that one of the toy dolls which past visitors had left for the little girl to play with had been moved from its usual position on top of the TV – it was now on the floor. Exactly how it had gotten there, none of them could say, but it had definitely not been there when they had first entered the room.

The next stop was Hank's room. Searching through the chest of drawers that contained his clothes, they found a box of matches in the second drawer from the top. One of the investigators took them and closed the drawer.

"If you'd like your matches back, Hank, all you have to do is open this drawer."

The team left and came back an hour later. The second drawer down was fully open. True to their word, the investigators replaced the matches. When they visited Hank's room later on that night, the unmistakable smell of cigarette smoke permeated the room. The odor was not attributable to any members of their team.

Next to the bathroom downstairs is a room used to store the Manor's I.T. equipment along with a bunch of other stuff. Twice that evening, the investigators reported sighting a floating white mass emerging from that room and disappearing into the hallway outside. Over in the nursing home wing, several of the visitors were touched on their arms and necks.

The next batch of visitors had quite the time in Hank's Room:

> *We went into Hank/Henry's room and messed with his clothes. Things were quiet until we left. 5 minutes after leaving the room, we captured a very loud and clear EVP disembodied voice telling us to 'GET OUT!'*
>
> *Before hearing this, we caught Hank's footsteps around the room, loud banging, and what seems to be a loud dragging sound. He was not happy. Mess with his clothes and he will come.*
>
> *Gracie's Room, we went into after Hank's. She warned us intelligently about Hank's anger upstairs, lighting the K-II meter sky high when asked questions.*

From the next group, still more nicotine odors were reported in Hank's Room, along with a very loud bang that the team were unable to satisfactorily explain and a glimpse of a shadow figure.

And so, the list goes on and on. Each time a fresh group of visitors comes to visit, they write their very own chapter in the ongoing story of the haunting of Malvern Manor. The guest books continue to expand, as eyewitness after eyewitness adds their own personal account of ghostly activity to the annals.

For every question that is answered, three more seem to arise. There really are no simple answers in cases such as this, and I suspect that Malvern Manor will continue to fascinate, frighten, infuriate, and delight visitors for many years to come.

Perhaps you will be one of them.

Acknowledgments

To the reader: Thank you for spending your hard-earned money and valuable time in order to read this book. It is my sincere hope that you have enjoyed it, and would ask you to **please** consider rating the book at the website it was purchased or borrowed from. In the current writing market, books tend to live and die by their reviews and ratings; your time would therefore be greatly appreciated.

Some very special thanks are due to the people without whom this book would not have been possible.

Stephen Weidner, Jill Woodward Saunderson, Erik Bensen, Connie Mianecki, and Susan Hatcliff, for inviting me to come along for the ride. You guys are the very best.

Big thanks are due to Josh Heard, for so many things; if

Josh hadn't said 'yes' to this project, than the book you have just finished reading would never have come into being in the first place. So thanks for everything, Josh...especially the shit tickets.

Sarah Stream, Jonah Jones, Kylie Fuller, and Amanda Borrego, thank you for sharing your experiences and theories. I hope to spend some time researching with you all in the not-so-distant future.

Johnny Houser, for graciously giving up his time to help...on date night, no less.

Dustin Pari, thanks for taking the time out of your busy schedule to share your reflections on not just Malvern Manor, but also the bigger picture.

The many people who have spent time investigating the haunting of Malvern Manor, and who have documented their experiences in the guest book.

Last, but by no means least, thanks are due to my wife

Laura.

Thank you all from the bottom of my heart – RE

Richard Estep
Longmont, Colorado
Richard@richardestep.net

The author on his first evening at Malvern Manor.

The rear of the structure, primarily the nursing home wing.

Rose, the haunted doll, likes to move around in her case at night.

Jill and Susan scoping out the second floor with the SLS camera

Josh discusses Malvern Manor's history with Stephen, Erik, and I

Stephen, Jill, and Susan doing some glass divination in the kitchen

Jill running a very laid-back EVP session in Gracie's room.

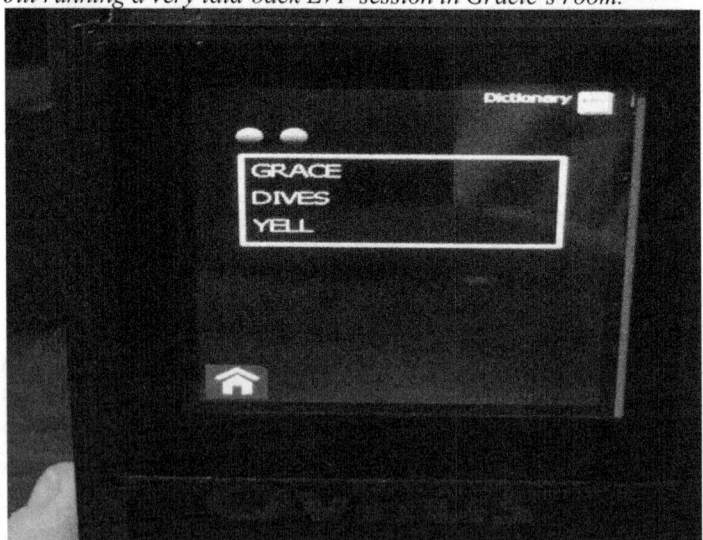

Ovilus hit from the doorway of Gracie's room.

We discover a pair of lost soles.

The author with Susan and Connie outside Room 2.

Printed in Great Britain
by Amazon

22296142R00175